The Denver Mint

100 Years of Gangsters, Gold, and Ghosts

The Denver Mint

100 Years of Gangsters, Gold, and Ghosts

By Lisa Ray Turner
and Kimberly Field

Mapletree Publishing Company
Denver, Colorado

Printed in the United States of America

11 10 09 08 07   1 2 3 4 5 6 7

Cover design by Tami Dever www.TLCGraphics.com

Library of Congress Cataloging-in-Publication Data

Turner, Lisa Ray.
  The Denver Mint : 100 years of gangsters, gold, and ghosts / by Lisa Ray Turner and Kimberly Field.
      p. cm.
  Includes bibliographical references and index.
  ISBN-13: 978-1-60065-102-1 (alk. paper) 1. Mints—Colorado—Denver—History. I. Field, Kimberly, 1957- II. Title.
HG461.D42T87 2006
338.7'6173749730978883—dc22
                                    2006012947   CIP

Printed on acid-free paper

Mapletree Publishing Company
Denver, Colorado 80130
800-537-0414
e-mail: mail@mapletreepublishing.com
www.mapletreepublishing.com
The Mapletree logo is a trademark of Mapletree Publishing Company

To my loving husband, Michael Field.—*Kimberly Field*

To the wonderful men in my life:
Robert, Devon, Ethan, and Bryce.—*Lisa Ray Turner*

About the Authors

Long-time Coloradan Kimberly Field holds a bachelor's degree in archaeology and a master's in journalism. Kim has written on western water issues, earthquake prediction and the influence of volcanoes in impressionist art. Her first introduction to the Denver Mint's products came with the shiny, Kennedy half dollars she received for each "A" on her report card.

Lisa Ray Turner is an award-winning writer of both fiction and nonfiction. She is the author of three novels, a book of essays (co-authored with Thomas S. Bollard) and many magazine articles for national publications. Lisa graduated with a bachelor's degree in education and received her master's degree in music. She teaches writing at Lighthouse Writers in Denver, and humanities at the University of Phoenix. Lisa is an avid coin collector. Unfortunately, as soon as she collects the coins, she spends them.

Table of Contents

Foreword

The Denver Mint. Thousands of tourists visit each year and watch, fascinated, as shiny copper pennies roll off the presses. Generations of school children have toured it and Denverites have been taking out-of-town guests to our Mint for a century. They proudly show off this Florentine money palace, a gorgeous building inspired by a Medici villa.

Many locals drive by the Mint on West Colfax every day with only a vague notion of what goes on inside. Denver shares the task of making all of the United States' circulating coinage with Philadelphia. Denver produces more than half of all U.S. pennies, nickels, dimes, quarters, half-dollars and dollar coins. All are branded with a "D."

During its first 100 years, many changes have rocked the Mint, but it has adjusted with the times. It expanded as Denver grew from a frontier mining supply town to a major metropolitan area. It adjusted coinage demands through two world wars, the Great Depression, and eighteen U.S. presidents. It survived a robbery attempt in the gangster-happy 1920s and changed the nation's coinage in response to the silver shortage of the 1960s.

Among the coins that have rolled off its presses are the beloved Lincoln penny and the Kennedy half-dollar, honoring two assassinated presidents. The 1964 Peace Dollar, the last true silver dollar, was produced in Denver and never circulated, one of the many strange stories in this book. Susan B. Anthony dollars are the first coins to bear a woman's image. In our own times, a new series of quarters tells each state's story in the embodiment of E Pluribus Unum, or "from many, one."

The city of Denver almost lost the Mint to the suburbs during the 1970s. Tightened security in the wake of the homegrown terrorism of the Oklahoma City bombing dismayed visitors who could no longer view the gold bars. Tours were abandoned after September 11, 2001, but once again are booming and easier than ever to arrange, with phone and online reservations. (Large groups may book tours by calling 303-405-4759. Individuals and families may reserve at www.usmint.gov.) The grand old landmark has been spruced up and modernized. As they have for a century, Denverites run the money-making machines, mop the floors, polish the coins and keep the country in change.

In *The Denver Mint: 100 Years of Gangsters, Gold, and Ghosts,* Kimberly Field and Lisa Ray Turner will take you through the Mint's first century with a lively look at one of Denver's most enduring treasures.

Tom (Dr. Colorado) Noel, professor of history,
University of Colorado at Denver

Acknowledgments

We had so much fun writing this book, especially meeting wonderful people who shared their passion for coins, Denver history and recollections of life in a bygone era. We thank everybody for their contributions.

Michael Field took many of the photographs in this book, and painstakingly formatted the entire collection for publication. We are grateful for his hours of work and cheerful attitude, even when shooting photos on a cold, windy winter day—and you know how the wind can roar down Colfax Avenue!

The employees of the US Mint, both in Denver and Washington DC, were invaluable to this project. All were a delight to work with.

The American Numismatic Association was a tremendous help. David Sklow, Nancy Green, and Amber Thompson of the Dwight N. Manley Library at the Money Museum in Colorado Springs were generous with their knowledge and time. The ANA's Lane J. Brunner, Ph.D., Erik J. Heikkenen, and Doug Mudd from the Money Museum, helped with research, photos and enthusiasm for our book.

Bob Akerley kindly shared his recollections of the Denver Mint, from when he walked past it each morning on his way to West High School in the 1930s. He also brought us materials from his extensive collection of Colorado historical documents and artifacts.

Glenna Goodacre and Daniel Anthony were gracious with their time, photographs, and insights into the design of the Golden Dollar.

The Western History Collection of the Denver Public Library was an incredible resource. Coi Gehrig in Photo Services uncovered unpublished Harry Mellon Rhoads' photos. Josie Teodosijeva in Photo Services and librarian Bruce Hanson in the Western History Department shared our thrill of discovery.

Julia Kanellos, historian at the Brown Palace Hotel contributed the recipe from a 1904 banquet at the hotel attended by Mayor Speer. Dozen's, a local breakfast institution, donated its award-winning Denver omelet recipe. Our friends were willing taste-testers.

Both the Colorado Historical Society and Historic Denver were of great help in this endeavor. Denver auditor Dennis Gallagher and Denver District Attorney Mitch Morrissey helped clarify Denver's relationship with the Mint. The Wednesday volunteers in the Anthropology Department of the Denver Museum of Nature and Science happily shared their recollections of life in Denver during World War II. Jim McNally found the newspaper article verifying the facts of the nickel-nicking incident.

The Writeous Sisters, our critique group of Jean Carey, Narcy Francone, and Martha Lederer, gave encouragement and constructive criticism and patiently read every word of our manuscript.

Tom "Dr. Colorado" Noel supported our efforts, and we hope he will be proud to include this book in his impressive collection of Colorado history.

Dave Hall and Sue Collier went above and beyond their call as publishers.

Kim Field's parents hoarded the silver coins we used in many of our photos. Our wonderful families read our manuscript and offered suggestions and general support. Any errors or omissions are solely our own.

Introduction: Money Makes the Mint Go 'Round

We love it, loathe it, and crave it. We use it every day. Most of the time, we simply want more of it.

Money.

Yet, with all the talk about the subject, we don't pay much attention to the actual coins and bills in our wallets and purses. We rarely think about where that money comes from.

Coins come to us courtesy of the US Mint. One of the most frequent questions to Denver Mint tour guides is, "Where do you make the dollar bills?" The Denver Mint doesn't print money. It only makes coins. Billions of them.

Despite the billions of coins that roll off the presses, most of us don't know much about mints. For example, did you know that George Washington supposedly donated some of his personal silver to the Mint to manufacture early coins? Or that the San Francisco Mint survived the great earthquake of

1906? Or that, according to a 1792 law, embezzlement by Mint employees is punishable by death?

Today's mints are just as interesting. The Denver Mint has grown from a small frontier operation to a world-class facility that produces 5 million quarters a day. If placed end to end, they would stretch over 75 miles long—or from the heart of Denver to the ski slopes of Copper Mountain. That's one day's production!

The next time you find a penny on the street, look for the tiny "D" marked on it and think about the Denver Mint.

"For a little penny or a dime, one can buy a lot of history."
—Eva Adams, director of the Mint (October 1961 to August
1969); from her statement on S. 1008 (repealing the
prohibition of mint marks) before the Senate Banking and
Currency Committee on May 2, 1967

CHAPTER ONE

The City Beautiful (1906–1920)

The City of Denver greeted the dawn of the twentieth century gussied up in the finest attire of the Victorian age. Her gown, if a bit vulgar, was of the costliest silk. Her bonnet was the latest Paris had to offer, although it was probably not the most tasteful. And her purse bulged with freshly mined gold from the abundant veins of the Rocky Mountains.

In the 1890s Denver was a lot like the woman who would become her most beloved legend. Molly Brown, whose heroics on the *Titanic* would forever dub her "unsinkable," had plenty of cash from her husband's mines in Leadville. But she was deemed too coarse for the salons of society. Molly eventually achieved her dreams of society's acceptance. Just like Molly, Denver never stopped trying. [1]

Denver had aspirations worthy of all that Gold Rush wealth. She would become the Queen City of the Plains. But an unpleasant relic of her frontier past stood in her way: the US Mint.

First, a Bit of History

During Colorado's gold rush of the 1860s, Denver was a rough settlement, more a collection of tents along Cherry Creek than the City Beautiful of which city fathers would later dream. Prospectors came down from their mining claims on Pikes Peak and Cripple Creek with leather pouches of gold dust, legal tender at the saloons, dry goods purveyors, and theaters of Denver. Miners would hold out their sacks for the bartender or merchant to take a pinch. It was a system that led to brawny fingers being the principal job requirement for Denver barkeeps.

Coins were needed. Clark, Gruber & Company [2] stepped up to begin minting gold coins in 1860, turning them out in weights trusted by miners and merchants and suitable for shipment to the East. The US government acquired the facility in 1863 and promptly expanded it. In 1864 it even provided safe haven to the Denver citizenry, who feared an Indian attack that failed to materialize. [3]

Then all upkeep and modernization stopped—at least that was the complaint of the burgeoning Denver newspapers by the late 1880s. Writers of the time decried the fortress-like brick building at Market and 16th Streets. One newspaper breathlessly declared that "to see this nondescript building in a city that has grown to become one of the chief cities of the nation causes a flush of indignation to mantle the cheeks of every true citizen of the nation."

Concern for the working conditions of Mint employees offered more grist for the Denver mill. The Mint sat below grade and formed a sump hole for "the corrupt seepage from the street." On a warm day or after a rain, an intolerable odor melding the worst of street garbage, horse droppings, and effluent from outhouses emanated from the site. Ill-lighted halls and grimy staircases contributed to the distasteful environment, and employees jammed into dark, cramped rooms akin to the mining shafts from which the gold originated. The Mint was so ugly that the Brotherhood of Locomotive Engineers apologized for its disgracefulness in its convention program.

Denver boasted thirty-one millionaires by 1890, many of whom were building grand, overwrought edifices in fancy neighborhoods far from the dirty streets of Denver's boom beginnings. One whiff of the sooty air confirmed the city's economic base of smelters and stockyards. Denver had more bars per capita than New Orleans, and down the block from the Mint, prostitutes advertised on garish signs complete

Visions of a City Beautiful: Looking east from the Denver Mint in the foreground, past the City and County Building and old Denver Library (now municipal offices) to the Colorado State Capitol, West Colfax presents the grand promenade of Mayor Robert W. Speer's City Beautiful. Famed Denver photographer Harry Rhoads captured this shot in about 1920 (top photo). It remains virtually unchanged over 75 years later (bottom photo). Photo Credit (historic photo): Denver Public Library Western History Collection. Photo Credit (contemporary photo): R. Michael Field.

with seductive pictures and suggestive messages. [4] The neighborhood of the old Denver Mint was the skid row Jack Kerouac would chronicle in *On the Road*. It would not see its renaissance until its lower downtown warehouses were turned to expensive lofts and trendy restaurants, and the area was dubbed LoDo nearly a century later.

In 1893 Denver real estate developer and political broker Robert Speer traveled to the World's Columbian Exposition in Chicago. He was taken by the White City, a neo-classical invocation of the City Beautiful movement sweeping American architecture. Speer imagined replacing the chaotic sprawl of young Denver with the ordered flow of imposing stone buildings capped with Greek pediments along broad, tree-lined boulevards promenading from a grand city center. It was a dream that would secure his election as mayor of Denver. Much of Denver's beauty today can be credited to Mayor Speer. [5]

A Grand Edifice Befitting a New Century

Denver's wish for a new Mint facility was granted with an 1895 congressional act that provided for a new Mint and the coinage of gold and silver. In 1899 ground was broken on West Colfax Avenue, within sight of the imposing Colorado State Capitol still under construction. Designed by James Knox Taylor to resemble the Palazzo Medici Riccardi in Florence, Italy, the new Mint would provide the west anchor of a grand civic center that would eventually be built.

The Denver newspapers soon took to grousing about the slow progress of construction, complaining that the Mint was nothing but a hole with a fence around it for the better part of two years. [6] Despite a state-of-the-art tramway for moving

The Denver Mint's Opening Strike: In 1905, this token was struck to test new coining machinery at the Denver Mint and, as some claim, to try out new dies for the $20 gold piece. It was distributed as a souvenir at ceremonies celebrating the start of coin production at the Denver Mint in the winter of 1906. The token was relatively scarce and completely unavailable later at the Mint. Too bad more lucky recipients didn't save their prize – it's now considered an extremely rare collectible. (Photo Credit: American Numismatic Association Money Museum)

huge granite blocks at the building site, construction delays dogged the project. Contractor J. A. McIntyre faced everything from encountering an old riverbed where he was supposed to put the foundation to the need for a granite quarry with sufficient quantities of the beautiful but rare granite chosen for the structure.[7] He dispatched what he described as "saucy" letters to his suppliers and subcontractors for blunders that were "enough to wreck the patience of an angel, not to say of a mint contractor." The Mint and the State Capitol relied on the same Chicago stone supplier. When a

The Good Old Lincoln Penny

Nearly five score years ago, the Denver Mint produced perhaps the most beloved, most collected, and certainly most numerous coin—the Lincoln penny. Radical in its time, it was the first coin to portray an actual person, let alone a president. George Washington set the no-presidents-on-coins precedent because appearing on a coin would be just the thing a king would do, and he was no king!

The Lincoln penny was the idea of another president—Teddy Roosevelt—to commemorate the one-hundredth anniversary of Lincoln's birth on February 12, 1809. The coin was instantly controversial upon its release in 1909. Was it the Lincoln profile that caused such consternation? Or the graceful stalks of wheat that simply graced its reverse? No, it was the initials—VDB! As was customary, designer Victor David Brenner placed his initials along the bottom rim of the reverse side. But critics considered the initials to be too large, an homage to himself rather than Lincoln. Within days the Treasury ordered the offending initials stricken, and the Mint produced an alternate variety of the 1909 Lincoln penny.

The very limited run of the 1909-S VDB made it the rarest of Lincoln pennies with fewer than 500,000 produced. Of course, collectors have been searching for them since 1909. Check your change—you might get lucky!

shipment of Italian marble intended for the State Capitol arrived at his site, McIntyre held it hostage until the supplier delivered his long-overdue shipment. [8]

The finished building was magnificent. An imposing red and gray granite structure of one hundred rooms, it was flanked by verdant lawns. Elaborate wrought iron grillwork barred its windows. The interior decoration spared little expense, with gray-veined white Vermont marble pilasters and panels. Wildly colored Tennessee marble surrounded the large classical windows. Vivid murals painted by Vincent Aderente depicting commerce, mining, and manufacturing

No Historic Building Is Complete Without a Ghost Story

On a rare foggy night in Denver, a church bell mournfully tolls midnight. A chill wind blows a few papers down a nearly deserted Colfax Avenue, and unusual sounds echo across the cavernous third floor of the Denver Mint. Welcome to the graveyard shift.

Seasoned Mint employees believe ghosts cause those thumps and thuds. At first it's easy to attribute the sounds to the settling of a century-old building. But sooner or later, as the hair on the back of your neck prickles one too many times, you come around.

One Mint employee, his coworker nodding somberly, recounts the story of the refrigerator: "We were on the third floor late one night. There is this old-fashioned refrigerator up there. As we were walking up to it, we watched the door open. Nobody opened it. There was nobody else there. It just opened by itself."

His coworker agrees that these are the facts of what they saw that night. "We went to shut it, of course. It was still perfectly cold, like the door had just opened. When we closed it, we realized it had a manual handle that you had to lift to open or close. So how did it open right in front of us?"

Of course, we can't say one way or another. But if you ever visit the Denver Mint and someone suggests you help yourself to a soda from the third floor fridge, we advise against it!

This recipe from the Brown Palace might have been popular in 1904, but most cooks today don't have this kind of time.

Roast Teal Duck au Cresson and Fried Hominy
(Courtesy of Brown Palace chefs)

Yield: 4 servings

Ingredients:
1 whole duck, preferably Maple Leaf
Mire poix (carrots, celery, onion)
   3 carrots (cut into 2-inch pieces)
   1 stalk celery (cut into 2-inch pieces)
   2 whole onions (yellow, rough chop)
1 bunch watercress
1 whole fresh lemon
1 tablespoon extra virgin olive oil
3 cups port wine
2 cups water
1 package grits (hominy)
Kosher salt, to taste
Fresh ground black pepper, to taste

Procedure:
Duck and Jus
   Rinse duck in cold water and pat dry with paper towels. Season the outside of the duck with salt and black pepper. Roast at 300 degrees Fahrenheit for 2 to 3 hours (depending on size of bird) on top of a bed of mire poix. When the bird is finished, set aside to rest. Deglaze the roasting pan with the port wine and a touch of water; this liquid is the sauce or jus. Put it in a large pot and simmer with the neck and other unneeded bones. While the bird rests, it will bleed juice; this is great to add to the jus. Remove the bones and strain out the mire poix if desired, or leave it in if vegetables are preferred. Then season with salt and fresh pepper.

(continued on next page)

Grits (Hominy)

In a large pot, simmer milk (slow-cooking grits are 4 parts liquid to 1 part grits; check the package for additional details or instructions). While simmering, whisk in grits quickly, reduce heat and continue to stir until cooked. Stir in salt and fresh pepper for seasoning. Oil a cookie tray lightly and spread the grits evenly on the tray. Then put the grits in refrigerator. When cool, cut out pieces to be floured and pan fried.

Watercress

Rinse and dry the watercress. Toss it with a squeeze of fresh lemon juice, a drizzle of olive oil, salt, and fresh pepper. Use this as a garnish.

Timing

Timing is paramount when cooking anything, especially this recipe. It will take about 4 to 5 hours to complete. The first step is to make and cool the grits. While they cool, start the bird. After the bird is cooked and resting, start the sauce or jus. When the sauce is finished, start the last minute preparations: frying the grits and dressing the watercress. For the grits, flour the pieces you cut and set aside. Heat oil over medium heat in a pot. When oil is hot enough, drop in the grits; they will cook rather quickly, in 2 to 4 minutes. While the oil is heating up, put the duck back in the oven for about 5 minutes at 350 degrees Fahrenheit to reheat it. As the grits fry, dress the watercress. When the grits are cooked and the bird is hot, the meal is ready.

graced the vaults of the main vestibule. Tiffany-style chandeliers lighted the polished corridors. Massive bronze doors at the Colfax Avenue entrance opened onto a flying double staircase at the center of the gallery.

The lavish facility, which at its essence is a factory, was completed in 1904 with cost overruns of 60 percent. [9] Coinage did not begin until 1906 because the machinery, the very latest in coin manufacturing, was displayed at the St. Louis Exposition during 1904.

At last Denver residents could be proud of their Mint. It quickly became a tourist attraction as visitors to the fledgling National Western Stock Show ogled the stately façade on their yearly visit to the big city. Denverites began a tradition that continues to this day—taking their children to see first-hand how money is made.

The Denver Mint set production records shortly after it opened. It produced 167 million coins in its inaugural year. For the first time in Denver, silver coins jangled from the presses along with twenty-dollar double eagle and ten-dollar eagle gold pieces. The Lincoln penny joined the ranks in 1909. During World War I, production ramped to a high that would not be equaled until America geared up to fight another world war.

The More Things Change, the More They Stay the Same

Like Molly Brown, the Mint remains dear to the hearts of Denver's citizenry. Its first century brought additions and renovations, and the Mint's exterior looked a little less like a bank with each. Fortunately, the City of Denver appreciated the unique charm of this unlikely factory, and it is now registered as a city and county landmark.

The opulence of the grand hall and gallery has been preserved. Today the gallery feels like a fine hotel straight out of the Victorian era. As your heels click on the worn marble, you may be tempted to examine the mottled, blood-red floor beneath your feet to assure yourself that it is real Italian marble and not the wild strokes of an artist's brush. The ochre-, moss-, and cream-colored tiles of the inlaid mosaic retain their brightness even after a century of use. The soft glow of Tiffany-style chandeliers warms the hushed, stone corridor with the burnished shine of century-old brass.

Every plaster surface around you is covered in the rich pallet of the Victorians. Terra cotta-colored walls rise to high vaulted ceilings resplendent with rose, olive, and deep mustard colors and finished with gold-painted crown molding. Even the ceiling of the flying staircase is beautifully painted, and the palatial feeling is only somewhat diminished by the machine gun nest where a Mint guard once sat with Tommy gun ready, a now empty relic of the 1920s.

Offices line the corridors, their heavy, varnished doors with large, frosted glass windows and transoms bespeaking a bygone era. Inside the offices the riot of color continues with elaborate crown molding whose egg and dart pattern echoes the decorated granite outside. The rich tones fashionable as the world entered the twentieth century adorn the walls, and heavy red drapes dress the tall windows. You might even glimpse an old-fashioned roll-top desk with a computer sitting on it.

The mezzanine, while still beautiful, reflects the challenge of running a modern factory in an antique space. Like a grand mansion converted into apartments, cubicles break up the spacious, old offices. Austere furniture and overhead fluorescent lighting accommodate the Mint's administrative employees. The information technology department graces an old office, filling it with utilitarian cubicles and gray plastic computer components.

If you look closely, high up on the walls of the gallery you might spot the brass teargas jets, standing by to deliver pepper spray in the new millennium. And that bump you hear coming from the third floor storage area just might be one of the ghosts rumored to walk the stately halls![10]

Chapter Notes

1. Louisa Ward Arps's excellent book *Denver in Slices* was our first stop for information about early Denver. The entire book is wonderful, and much of the information about the unsinkable Molly Brown can be found here. Complete references for this book, and all materials we used in our research, can be found in the bibliography.

2. Our book deals with the "new" Denver Mint facility that recently celebrated its one-hundredth birthday. We refer fleetingly to Clark, Gruber & Company, predecessor of the modern Denver Mint. The story of that facility is covered in *Denver in Slices*, particularly "Slice 5, Gold Coins in Denver Mints."

3. Bob Akerley, who has been at the Denver Museum of Nature and Science for more than sixty years, provided information on the Clark, Gruber & Company facility, including an article from the July 1957 issue of *The Denver Westerners Monthly Roundup*.

4. Phil Goodstein's *The Seamy Side of Denver* provided the information about the prostitutes of Market Street.

5. *Denver, the City Beautiful and Its Architects, 1893–1941*, by Thomas J. Noel and Barbara S. Norgren was a tremendous resource to us. Dr. Noel, also known as "Doctor Colorado," has authored many books about Denver and Colorado history. The chapter on Robert Speer and the City Beautiful contains a wealth of information on turn-of-the-century Denver and how the City Beautiful Movement influenced Mayor Speer.

6. Much of the information reported in the Denver newspapers was found in the collection of the Western History Department of the Denver Public Library. The clippings are old, mostly tiny, yellowed shreds without

the newspaper's name or date it was published. The librarians have filed them under "Denver Mint Administration" by decade.

7. Platte Canyon red granite, quarried near Buffalo Creek in neighboring Jefferson County, provides a stout foundation for the Mint. When construction began, Cotopaxi granite, a fine-grained gray stone, was used for the main structure. However, the vein formation of Cotopaxi did not produce the uniform stone in quantities necessary for the Mint. J. A. McIntyre located a source of the granite near Arkins in Larimer County, north of Denver. The stone occurred in block formation, which was more suitable for building. Soon the quarry, conveniently located 2 miles from the Loveland spur of the Colorado & Southern Railroad, yielded three railcars a day of fine granite, which a small army of stonecutters worked on at the site.

8. There are conflicting reports of what stone was used in the 1904 Denver Mint building. We relied on news accounts from the time of construction and Jack Murphy's *Geology Tour of Denver's Buildings and Monuments* (Historic Denver, Inc. and Denver Museum of Natural History, 1995, pages 6-21, 28-29). Jack Murphy is curator emeritus of geology at the Denver Museum of Nature and Science. His geologic tour offers an interesting and fun look at Denver's historic buildings.

9. For construction costs we consulted the Annual Report of the Director of the Mint for the fiscal year ending June 30, 1906, pages 6-7.

10. Our description of the Grand Hallway and other interiors of the Denver Mint come from our tour with Guillermo Hernandez, public affairs director at the Denver Mint. He is justifiably proud of that magnificent building. For the

record, he said there are no ghosts. But we heard
differently from many unnamed sources!

CHAPTER TWO

Crime and Punishment at the Denver Mint (1920–1930)

H as the Mint ever been robbed?" Tourists often ask Mint tour guides this question. The only question asked more often is, "Do we get free samples at the end of the tour?"

There are no free samples. But robberies? Yes. Two notorious heists happened in the twenties. The first was an inside job, the second a bit more dramatic.

The Wooden Leg Robber

Orville Harrington was about as far from the image of a twenties gangster as you can get. There were no guns hidden in a violin case or double-breasted, pinstriped suit for this recluse, who rarely left home except to go to work. He was a quiet sort who dutifully worked eight hours a day at the Denver Mint and spent his weekends puttering around his Washington Park bungalow or tending zinnias in his garden. Orville was married to Lydia Harrington, a petite woman who seemed as satisfied at home as her husband, content with raising two children, canning fruit, and tending chickens.

Orville's only distinguishing feature was his uneven gait and the way his body sagged to one side when he walked. He'd been shot in the hip during a hunting accident when he was eleven, and the incident doomed him to a lifetime of pain. His leg was amputated two years after the accident, and he had worn a wooden leg since that time. Therein lies the tale—and maybe the gold.

Orville was a long-time, trusted employee in the Mint refinery; he had not, however, set out to become a Mint worker. By all accounts a highly intelligent man, he'd graduated from the Colorado School of Mines, where he'd trained to be a mining engineer. Despite graduating with honors from both high school and college, he couldn't get an engineering job; society's attitudes about disabilities were unenlightened in the twenties, to say the least. Orville reluctantly accepted a factory job at the Mint.

Orville made $4 a day, with a monthly bonus of $20. Yet each day he handled shiny bricks of gold worth vast amounts of money. Of course, it's impossible to know what went through his head, but he likely felt frustrated by the knowledge that he'd never make much more than $4 a day and that his job prospects were limited by his disability. Whatever the reason, Orville began walking out of the Mint with gold bars, one bar per day.

He planned the embezzlement well, timing the thefts in the interval between inventories. Using this rationale, he could have tucked away thousands of dollars worth of gold and nobody would have known which of the thirty-nine refinery employees had stolen the gold bars.

He even devised a plan to use the gold. Since it would be difficult, if not impossible, to sell a large quantity of gold, he planned to lease an abandoned mine near Victor, Colorado, melt the gold and claim he'd mined it. Gold was still being mined in Colorado, so this could have worked, although it sounds ludicrous today. Over a five-month period, Orville managed to steal fifty-three bars of gold alloy, worth $81,400. Adjusted for inflation, that would be about $828,000.[1]

How does someone walk out of the Mint with a bar of gold? In today's high-security environments, where cameras lurk in the corners of every building from 7-Elevens to massive government structures, it's hard to imagine. But Orville lived in a simpler time, before metal detectors, x-ray scans, and the like. Still, the bars he stole were not small coins or nuggets that could easily be pocketed. They were seven inches by three inches and one-inch thick. Each weighed around eight pounds. Just how did he accomplish this feat?[2]

A Woman of Her Time

Lydia Harrington is described as a small woman with dark, curly hair. She was educated and had worked as a nurse. She was devoted to home, Orville, and their two young children, who were both seriously ill at the time of Orville's arrest. She kept an immaculate home, grew vegetables, and tended a flock of white chickens in the backyard.

As was the case with most women in the twenties, Lydia's heart was firmly attached to home and hearth, but when Orville went to prison she had to pay the bills. She wanted to keep the house so Orville could return to it—and her—after he'd served his time. She got a job as a nanny for a wealthy Denver family and put her own children in an orphanage so she could work. She moved from her beloved home to the tiny chicken house in the backyard.

This could be the stuff of a three-hankie movie, complete with devoted wife, loving children, and the repentant husband who returns home after paying his debt to society, having learned his lessons and bearing gratitude for the forgiving wife who stood by his side. But this was real life.

Orville served three and one-half years of his sentence, was released early, and returned to Lydia. They moved back into their lovely house with their now healthy children. From the outside, it appeared that the Harringtons' problems were behind them. Orville resumed his place as head of the family and got a job working for the City of Denver.

A short three years later, Orville quit his job and told Lydia he planned to go to Arizona to seek out better job opportunities. He left her and the children behind and went his own way.

Undoubtedly, Lydia was devastated to be left alone again, but things only got worse for her. It wasn't long before various friends reported they'd seen Orville around town. Apparently, he never made it to Arizona. This seems like the ultimate cruelty—to abandon Lydia after she'd been so devoted. But that's exactly what Orville did. The couple split up and went their separate ways. Orville never got the wealth, good health, comfortable home, or happy family he had wanted. He didn't even get the notoriety that other criminals of the time received.

If Only

Harry Barnes was an orphan in the 1920s, sent to live with an aunt when his mother succumbed to tuberculosis. He made friends quickly in his new Washington Park neighborhood and delighted in hearing tales about the infamous Wooden Leg Robber of the Denver Mint. A special appeal lay in his proximity to the crime—legend had it that he lived right down the street from the notorious crook.

As the Depression deepened in Denver, Harry and his friends would sneak into their neighbor's yard under the cover of darkness, searching for the gold they were sure was there. These daring, midnight raids continued until he went off to the Army.

Denied his piece of the plunder, Harry married, built a career, and raised a family. Decades later, he discovered that he had been digging in the wrong backyard. [4]

This is where accounts from the time period vary. Some claim Orville hid the gold bars in the hollow chamber of his wooden leg. [3] Others claim Orville simply carried the bars in his pockets or hid them beneath his jacket. In either event, his prosthetic leg contributed to his ability to commit the crime. Orville was a large man, and the leg caused him to slump and limp when he walked, so his body position would have disguised a gold bar tucked away in his clothing.

Orville hid the gold in his cellar, behind shelves bulging with tidy jars of canned fruit, and buried more under a concrete walkway in his yard. Eventually, Orville's creative crime spree ended when a fellow employee, who suspected him of the crime, alerted the authorities. Rowland K. Goddard, supervising agent for the Secret Service in Denver, shadowed Orville and confronted him February 4, 1920, as Orville was leaving work for the day. Orville confessed to the crime and showed Goddard where he'd hidden the gold. Orville was promptly arrested, tried, and sentenced to ten years in prison.

News of her husband's crime stunned poor Lydia. She thought he was merely a good handyman. In the February 8, 1920, issue of the *Rocky Mountain News*, she said, "[I] saw him digging in the garden, as if people don't dig in the garden in the spring. ... They said they found gold out there last night, but I do not believe it. I do not believe they found it anywhere."

Orville and Lydia's house was razed in the fifties when the Valley Highway was built. Folks poked around the old homestead, wondering if the Secret Service could have neglected a gold bar here or there. But none was ever found. [5]

The Great Mint Robbery

The roaring twenties. Those words evoke images of homemade gin flowing in backyard stills, scarlet-lipped flappers dancing the Charleston, and black Model Ts chugging down city streets. It was, indeed, a time of transformation. The twenties produced the first transatlantic

Prohibition Punch

7 to 8 cups frozen, unsweetened strawberries
1 6-ounce container frozen limeade concentrate
1 cup pineapple juice
2 liters lemon-lime beverage (7-Up or Sprite; diet drinks or Fresca can also be used)

Thaw frozen strawberries. Do not drain. Blend berries in a blender or food processor until they're smooth and liquefied. Put berries into a pitcher or punch bowl. Add limeade and pineapple juice. Chill until ready to serve. Right before serving, add carbonated beverage and ice. Garnish with lime slices, strawberries, and fresh mint leaves.

Note: This tastes suspiciously like a strawberry daiquiri, despite the lack of alcohol. We imagine twenties bootleggers would toss in a cup of rum.

flight, jazz, and the Miss America Pageant. Women got to vote, then shortened their skirts and bobbed their hair. Prohibition began in 1920, spawning speakeasies and a bootlegging trade that thrived throughout the decade.

The twenties also gave birth to organized crime. The names Bugsy Malone, Lucky Luciano, and Al Capone became as well known as Charlie Chaplin and Al Jolson. The cigar-puffing gangster in a pinstriped suit—submachine gun in hand and beautiful woman at his side—embodied the time.[6]

It's no surprise the Mint was robbed during this time period. However, it must be said that *technically* the Mint was not robbed. The gangsters never got inside the fortress-like Mint building. Their target: a Federal Reserve truck that was parked in front of it.

On December 18, 1922, workers were transferring five-dollar bills from the Mint into a truck that was parked outside the front entrance. The money was stored in vaults leased by the Federal Reserve inside the Mint. A black Buick touring car roared up and screeched to a stop. Two masked men with sawed-off shotguns jumped from the car and yelled, "Hands up!" Other robbers shattered the truck window and snatched the packets of money. A getaway driver was hunched behind the wheel of the Buick, ready to barrel away when the job was done.

Chaos erupted. Outside, one guard bolted for the protection of a parked car, since his gun had tumbled to the ground. Another dropped the $100,000 he was carrying and dodged bullets by diving under the money truck. Another sprinted back inside the building. Guard Charles T. Linton fired his revolver. A shot from the gunmen shattered the air. Linton collapsed, blood gushing from his body.

Inside the Mint alarms shrieked. According to Allen Webb, the guard who tripped the alarm, it was difficult for

Mint guards to distinguish the bandits from the guards. A fierce gun battle ensued. Mint workers later counted fifty-one bullet holes in the door of the Mint and thirty-seven in the paneling. Stray bullets were also lodged in apartments and businesses in the surrounding area. [7]

The bloody affair was over in ninety seconds. The robbers got away with $200,000—the equivalent of $2 million in today's money. Witnesses tell how a bandit with blood dripping from his hand stopped to snatch a bundle of money that had been dropped on the street. He tossed the money in the car, leaped in, and yelled, "Let's go!"

The Buick zoomed away from the Mint. It slammed into a fire hydrant and water spewed into the air, but the vehicle kept moving. The getaway car then sideswiped a truck but kept going. It gained momentum as it screeched past the Capitol building and down Colfax. A police car chased them, but the thugs got away.

City officials quickly set up roadblocks on every road leading out of Denver, and sheriff departments in surrounding counties were notified. Policemen pursued one suspicious car heading out of town, but when they stopped it, they discovered its occupants were only bootleggers with whiskey. The city offered a ten-thousand-dollar reward for the capture of the crooks. Dead or alive, it didn't matter.

Despite these efforts, the Buick could not be found. Only one clue was left behind in the aftermath of the sensational crime: a bloodied shotgun.

Back at the Mint, the most immediate impact of the crime was pandemonium. Crowds of onlookers thronged the grounds and building, while mounted police attempted to maintain order. Reports from witnesses conflicted wildly. They didn't agree on the number of gangsters or how the robbery transpired. They gave eight different license numbers for the getaway car. Only two details remained consistent, that two of the gunmen appeared to be wounded and the getaway car was a black Buick touring car.

Within two hours of the crime, Mint guard Charles Linton died. The gunmen had now committed murder and robbery. Denver police launched the largest manhunt in Denver history and federal officers within a 400-mile radius were ordered to be on the lookout for the robbers. Almost every Denver police officer was put on the job. Rowland K.

The Copyboy Saw It All

In 1922 Paul Clar was a lowly copyboy at the now-defunct *Denver Express* newspaper. In today's parlance, he'd be called a go-fer.

On the day of the robbery, one of his bosses asked Paul to fetch rolls and coffee from the Mint Café. The cafe was directly across from the Mint, and as Paul walked inside, he noticed a black Buick touring car pulling up to the Mint's entrance. Within seconds Paul heard the blast of the first shot. Terrified, he crouched behind a tree in front of the cafe. From that vantage point, he watched the robbery. He saw it all—the murder of the guard and wounding of one of the robbers, the flying bullets, the swarm of guards fleeing the Mint.

After the bandits drove away, Paul sped back to the *Express* offices and yelled at one of the editorial assistants, "The Mint's been robbed!" The assistant didn't believe him. Paul insisted that the Mint had indeed been robbed and that he'd witnessed it. Again, the assistant pooh-poohed the story. Paul was only a copyboy, after all.

Paul was reportedly so irritated by the assistant's smug attitude, he jumped on his bicycle and pedaled to the offices of the competing newspaper, the *Denver Post*, where an editor took down his story and published it. By the time Paul returned to the *Express* offices, the *Post's* afternoon edition was circulating, with blazing headlines about the robbery. The top dogs at the *Express* wanted to fire Paul. But when Paul told what had happened, they fired the editorial assistant instead. [8]

Denver Enters the Gangster Era: Mint robber J. S. Sloane, aka Nicholas Trainor. His body was found frozen in the car shown in a garage on Gilpin Street in Denver a month after the robbery. The guns on the left were found in the car. (Photo Credit: Denver Public Library Western History Collection)

Denver's Crime of the Century Planned at the Altahama Apartments: The Altahama Apartments on Colfax Avenue was home to several of the gang that robbed the Denver Mint. Here, the day of the robbery, December 18, 1922, is spelled out in this photo of the era: (1) 8 A.M., the gang meets to have breakfast and finalize plans; (2) around 9 A.M., the men of the gang left the apartment in a stolen car; (3) male voices were heard in the apartment between noon and 1 P.M.—they were thought to be dividing the loot before hightailing it out of town; and (4) Mrs. J. S. Sloan, widow of the slain robber (whose frozen corpse had yet to be found by police) left the apartment building around 3 P.M. two days after the robbery. Accompanied by Mr. and Mrs. Harold G. Burns, the trio carries suitcases assumed to carry their share of the loot. An arrow points to the windows of the apartment in which the gang lived, which are circled in the photo. (Photo Credit: Denver Public Library Western History Collection)

Honoring a Thief: Denver turned out in force to attend the funeral of Mint robber J. S. Sloan. Scores of men volunteered to be pall bearers, and ladies swooned as he was laid to rest at Riverside Cemetery. (Photo Credit: Denver Public Library Western History Collection)

Bandit Queen: Florence Thompson (alias Florence Sloan) abandoned her husband and small child to take up with J. S. Sloan, aka Nicholas Trainor. One report claimed her bullet-riddled corpse was found near Minneapolis in 1927. Secret Service agents believed they located her in Chicago in 1930, but did not arrest her. In 1932, she and Maggie Shecog (alias Mrs. Harold Burns) were supposedly found shot, daubed with battery acid and burned to death in Wisconsin, although some reports state vehemently that Florence Sloan's was not among the bodies found. (Photo Credit: Denver Public Library Western History Collection)

Goddard, the head of the Secret Service in Denver and the same man who had apprehended Orville Harrington, became fixated on finding the killers.

Evidence was scanty. Even the best clue—the bloody gun—couldn't be used for fingerprints because too many people had touched it. The police checked area hospitals, but nobody with gunshot wounds had checked into them. An extensive manhunt rendered no leads. Rewards totaling $15,000—huge for the time—were offered, but no one came forward. Tips came in, but they didn't lead to any substantive suspects. Most were flimsy, such as the dry cleaner who reported cleaning a bloody suit, only to find out its owner had been in a weekend brawl.

Anxiety engulfed Denver. The price of alcohol, illegal because of Prohibition, shot up since hyper-vigilant policemen became so efficient at hunting bootleggers. Shoppers, banks, and businesses rejected five-dollar bills for fear of being linked to the robbery.

Rumors spread through the city. Sightings of robbers were reported from Greeley, Colorado, to Baltimore, Maryland, and points in between. Detectives speculated that there were twelve robbers instead of five, some disguised as policemen. Officials wondered whether the same outlaws who'd robbed a bank in Kansas City a week earlier had committed the crime. A waitress bragged that she was *intimately* associated with one of the bandits. A young man announced he was one of the robbers, but his claims were quickly proven false and he was whisked away to an asylum. A psychic predicted that one of the gangsters would yell out his confession in a Christmas church service after placing a stolen five-dollar bill in the collection plate.

The police were completely stymied until January 14, 1923, when their big break came. Acting on a tip from a man who was suspicious of a new, sturdy padlock on his neighbor's abandoned garage, they found the Buick at 1631 Gilpin Street. The police were in for an even greater shock when they searched the Buick. The dead body of one of the bandits was inside, frozen solid!

Bullets had penetrated his hand, wrist, and heart. He was obviously the robber with the bleeding hand that several witnesses had reported seeing. Cartridge shells were strewn on the floor of the Buick, and a loaded shotgun sat on the back seat. Dried blood mottled the outside of the doors.

Only one problem remained: Who was the dead guy? The detectives didn't recognize him by sight, and his fingers were so shriveled they couldn't run fingerprints. A photo of the dead man's face was published in the *Denver Post* with the heading, "Who is this man?" Finally, in an effort to discover his identity, the police peeled the man's skin away from his fingertips and stretched it over police officers' fingertips to get prints. They learned his name was Nick Trainor, alias J. R. Sloan. A convicted felon, he had just been paroled from the Nebraska State Penitentiary.

The discovery of Trainor's body increased the frenzy in Denver. Florence Thompson, Trainor's so-called bandit queen, provided much of the intrigue. Florence was a former prostitute who'd abandoned her husband and young son to travel with Trainor. When a spray of carnations arrived at the undertaker's parlor the night before Trainor's funeral with an anonymous note asking that it be placed on his casket, Florence was the suspected sender. A couple of days prior, Florence had reportedly gone to the funeral home in a disguise. Newspaper accounts reported the mystery woman's demeanor: "Her fists were clenched, straight by her side. She stopped. For a long moment she stood there, rigid.... Then one hand was raised to her lips, as if to stifle a sob.... She glanced fearfully over one shoulder. She wrung her hands. Abruptly, panic seemed to overwhelm her. Again she turned.

Again she fled. She has not been seen since."

A local undertaker donated a casket in which to bury Trainor. Since this was the twenties, gangsters were as popular as movie stars, and many men clamored to be pallbearers. Trainor was buried at Riverside Cemetery, his burial paid for from public funds.[9]

Drama aside, finding Trainor's body was a significant development. It validated a tip the police had received just a few days after the robbery when a woman reported the questionable activity of her neighbors, James and Florence Sloan. When the police checked on the lead, they found that the Sloans—Nick Trainor and Florence—had deserted an apartment, leaving Christmas gifts and clothing behind. The Sloans had also left behind a bank receipt that showed Florence had used a false name to withdraw $1,500 from a Denver bank a few days before the robbery.

The police had also received word that on the afternoon of the robbery, suspicious voices were heard in an apartment house at 1310 East Colfax Avenue. This was actually the place where the gang had planned the robbery. The police also verified that the gang had gathered there to divide the money. Florence and another of the bandit's wives had also been present.

At the same time this lead came in, the police had received a tip from a different neighbor about another couple, Harold and Margaret Burns. The neighbor reported that a mysterious steamer trunk had been delivered to the Burns. Detectives found the steamer trunk, but it was empty except for a few photos (of the Sloan and Burns couples). The two couples had come to Denver months before the robbery. They lived a high life even though they had no obvious means of support. The police had suspected their involvement in the robbery. Now with the discovery of the getaway car and Trainor's body, the link was clear.

This was a good start to solving the case, but progress was slow, the work painstaking. Rowland K. Goddard,[10] supervisor of the Secret Service in Denver for more than forty years, embraced the challenge of finding the perpetrators. Goddard never lost his zeal for the case.

He and his colleagues learned that several gangs from St. Paul, Minnesota, had joined to pull the Denver Mint robbery. Following leads from St. Paul, a city notorious for money laundering, where the cash had been offered to bankers for laundering, Goddard and crew pieced together the names of the gangsters, although the names weren't made public. Identification of criminals was difficult in those days. Social Security numbers and modern record keeping didn't exist, so it was easy for lawbreakers to simply change their names, and most adopted numerous aliases during their careers. Although it was difficult to get a clear picture of the gangsters, the following were implicated in the robbery:

♦ Harvey Bailey (alias Big Jim Franklin)—Bailey has been called the "dean of the American bank robbers." He was the most successful bank robber of his day and got away with over a million dollars during his illustrious career. Bailey never admitted his part in the robbery.

♦ Robert Leon Knapp (alias Harold Burns)—Knapp was a robber from Michigan who was wanted for robbery and the murder of two policemen.

♦ Maggie Shecog (Burns's mistress, alias Margaret Burns)— Knapp's "bandit queen," Shecog was a Native American from the Chippewa tribe who had started traveling with Knapp after being expelled from the reservation for prostitution.

♦ James Clark—A renowned criminal, he eventually served a life term in the Indiana State Penitentiary after a 1930 robbery of a bank in Indiana. Like Bailey, he never admitted to his part in the Denver Mint crime.

- Nicholas Trainor (alias J. S. Sloan)—Originally involved in criminal activity in Ireland, Trainor became entangled in the American crime scene in St. Paul. His life of crime ended when he was killed during the Mint robbery.

- Florence Thompson (alias Florence Sloan) —Trainor's bandit queen. The gang originally promised her Nick's share of the loot since he was killed during the crime. They reneged on that promise. Florence called on Thomas Bell, a notorious bank robber, and Bell successfully forced the gang to pay up.

- Otto Schulz—Not directly involved in the robbery, Schulz was a small-time bootlegger who knew the robbers and ended up aiding the investigation—and keeping himself out of prison—by giving information.

Other names were bandied about, and some detectives speculated that there were as many as twelve robbers and two or three women. Progress on the case remained slow. It was over a year later, in February 1923, that Goddard and other agents laid an elaborate plan to trap the bandits.

A Cincinnati banker reported that he'd been offered $80,000 of the Denver Mint money during a trip to St. Paul. Goddard and other agents assembled in St. Paul, knowing that if the money was there, the robbers couldn't be far behind. Their plan seemed foolproof, as they worked with postal inspectors, bankers, bootlegger Otto Schulz, and underworld figures to set up the operation. The investigators' excitement level ran high—too high. The Cincinnati banker was agog about his involvement in the adventure, and he spilled the proverbial beans to people in St. Paul. His story made newspaper headlines, and the project blew up in Goddard's face.

The investigation never gained the same level of energy, although $80,000 of the money was recovered in St. Paul in 1923. Years passed. Witnesses moved away. Trails ran cold. Nobody was ever charged in the great Denver Mint Robbery

Twelve years after the crime, the Denver Police Department announced that the case had been solved because everybody connected with it was either dead or in prison. Frank McFarland and Robert Knapp were dead. Harvey Bailey was serving a life sentence in Alcatraz for kidnapping. James Clark was in prison in Indiana, and both bandit queens[11] had been murdered. Otto Schulz lived in California and had no more information to share about the crime.

The crime is now relegated to dusty history books and faded newspapers. It remains the most sensational robbery in Denver, a vestige of a bloody crime wave that flourished in the United States as the twenties roared into the history books as well. It's a safe bet that the Mint will never be robbed again, given its ironclad security. Two words for anyone who'd like to attempt it: Fuhgeddabout it! [12]

Chapter Notes

1. The Bureau of Labor Statistics Website, http://
www.bls.gov / offers information on the changing value
of money. We used its Inflation Calculator to adjust
dollars to today's values.

2. The newspapers of the 1920s provide an illuminating look
into the crimes discussed in Chapter Two. The headlines
from the February 6, 1920, issue of the *Rocky Mountain
News* are shocking to modern readers: "Cripple Admits
Guilt; Tells How He Carried Gold in Artificial Leg."
Another article begins with this flowery language:
"Dazed and crushed by the tragedy which has suddenly
entered and upset the serenity of her secluded household,
Mrs. Orville Harington [sic] believes there is nothing she
can say concerning the guilt of her husband. ..." The word
"alleged" doesn't appear in any of the articles about
Harrington.

3. The *Denver Post*'s February 5, 1920, issue published a
sketch of Harrington's artificial leg.

4. Mrs. Karen Purley shared her childhood dreams of being
a little rich girl—if only her father had been digging in the
right backyard!

5. Rumors persisted that Orville Harrington's home was
bulldozed to make way for the Valley Highway.
Published reports to this effect appeared in Pasquale
Marranzino's column in the August 4, 1954, issue of the
Rocky Mountain News and Alice Spencer Cook's story in
the November 13, 1966, *Empire* magazine (supplement to
Denver Post). The city directory of 1920, however, lists
Harrington's address as further north on University than
the highway construction. By the late 1950s, Orville's
address had been deleted from the city plat.

6. The culture of the twenties played an important part in the Great Denver Mint Robbery of 1922. Here are a few of the excellent Web sites about the twenties that we used: http://webtech.kennesaw.edu/jcheek3 roaring _twenties.htm; http://www.crimelibrary.com/ gangsters_outlaws/gang/harlem_gangs/2.html; http:// www.nfatoys.com/tsmg/web/twenties.htm; http:// www.historylearningsite.co.uk/1920s_America.htm; http://history1900s.about.com/od/1920s/a/flappers. htm

7. Long-time Colorado resident and history buff Bob Akerley shared many insights about the Denver Mint and the city before World War II. He described watching the construction of the Mint addition and gold vaults in the 1930s as he walked to class at West High School. He told us where on the granite façade we might find bullet holes from the Great Mint Robbery. We've got to be honest, however; we looked but never really saw them. We did see the scars in the marble in the Grand Hallway from the flying bullets. Look for missing chunks at about eye level at the intersection of the Grand Hallway and entry vestibule.

8. The story of copyboy Paul P. Clar was reported in the May 29, 1959, issue of the *Denver Post* and a December 18, 1960, issue of the *Denver Post* (the thirty-eighth anniversary of the Mint robbery).

9. It may be difficult to grasp the public's fascination with criminals during the twenties. The high degree of interest in the Denver Mint robbery and Trainor's funeral show that residents of Denver were as enthralled with crime as the rest of the country.

10. Rowland K. Goddard began working for the Secret Service on December 1, 1901, and came to Denver in 1906.

On November 7, 1907, he was named supervising agent of the Denver office. In November 1941, years after the Denver police closed the robbery case in 1934, he said in a *Rocky Mountain News* article, "There have been plenty of real cases in Denver during my 35 years. But the fact that we never got any of those men who pulled the Mint robbery makes it the most outstanding." Goddard became one of the country's leading experts on counterfeiting. He died in 1949. Interviews with Goddard about the Harrington robbery appeared in the *Denver Post* (August 13, 1933, and August 19, 1945) and the *Rocky Mountain News* (August 21, 1945, and October 22, 1946).

11. The bandit queens of the twenties are endlessly fascinating and a sad footnote to the gangster era. We researched the bandit queens for the Denver Mint Robbery in the following two articles: "The Great Denver Mint Robbery" by John Snyder in the *Empire Magazine* and "Five Hit Mint in Bold, Bloody '22 Heist" by Marjie Lundstron in the May 26, 1985, issue of the *Denver Post*.

12. Information about the Denver Mint robbery of 1922 came largely from the local newspapers from 1922 and a retrospective article published in the *Denver Post* on May 26, 1985. The quote about Florence Thompson's behavior comes from an excellent retrospective article on the crime from the May 26, 1985, *Denver Post*. Details of the hunt for the robbers are from the *Rocky Mountain News*, January 15, 1984, Frances Melrose's column, "Rocky Mountain Memories."

CHAPTER THREE

Show Me the Gold (1930–1940)

The word gold is synonymous with wealth, goodness, and status. Obedient children are good as gold. A compassionate person has a heart of gold. An efficient housekeeper is worth her weight in gold. Athletes win gold medals; singers yearn for gold records. If you have a good credit rating you get a gold card. And if you're lucky, you'll celebrate your golden anniversary in your golden years.

Gold is the stuff of legends, mythology, and adventure. King Midas of Greek and Roman mythology lost his daughter because of his obsession with gold. The Queen of Sheba exchanged gifts of gold for King Solomon's wisdom. Coronado searched the desert southwest for the fabled Seven Cities of Gold. He should have waited five hundred years and gone to Denver.

The Denver Mint has always been associated with gold. In fact, part of the reason the Mint came to Denver was the 1858 Colorado gold rush. The Clark & Gruber Assay office— the forerunner for the Denver Mint—opened to fill the need for coinage.

Gold is still king today. Enormous vaults in the Mint store gold bars. Most employees never see the bars, and very few handle them. Although the exact amount is kept secret, some say the Mint stockpiles one-fourth of the country's gold; others claim the amount is closer to one-half.

Why does Denver have so much gold? To answer that question, we'll go back to an early time in the Mint's history: 1908. At that time the San Francisco Mint stored $270 million in gold—that's over $5 billion today. The San Francisco Mint's vaults were inadequate, and Mint Director Frank Leach[1] feared robbers would tunnel into the vaults and rob them, especially after overhearing two men discuss such a

Melding the Old With the New: This 1936 addition to the Denver Mint is faithful to the original building with its use of granite and similar design. The addition, however, lacks the depth of detail. (Photo Credit: R. Michael Field)

caper one night at a theater. He also was afraid the gold could fall into enemy hands in the event of war.

At that time, the Denver Mint was new, its vaults shiny and strong and equipped with first-rate security. With the San Francisco's 1906 earthquake still in mind, Denver's geological stability gave added appeal. More important, Denver was inland. Enemies would have to travel a thousand miles across the country to get to it. It was an ideal place to store the gold.

But how to move such massive heaps of money? Today we move money with a few clicks at the computer. But moving stacks of gold bars is a different story. Gold is heavy and unwieldy. Hiding a couple of elephants would be easier than concealing gold coins worth $270 million.

In San Francisco a large force of specially trained workers handled the gold. They weighed canvas bags, which each held $5,000 in coins, then packed them in pine boxes. Each box weighed 140 pounds.

The Sweeps Cellar

Did you know the Mint used to save its dirt? It's true! Most of us have far more dirt than we need, so why would the Mint salvage it?

Gold, that's why. Prospectors have always found gold by sifting and washing loose dirt. Given the amount of gold in the Mint, it's not surprising that the Mint would do the same thing.

In the early decades of the Mint's existence, employees swept every stray speck of dirt into the cellar, then packed it into sacks. Small bits of silver, nickel, copper—and yes, gold—ended up in those bags, along with the dregs. Dust from precious metals was even culled from water used for employee showers. The sweeps cellar bags were sold each year. [2]

Today the only gold dust at the Mint is inside the vaults in the form of gold bars. The old sweeps cellar is still there, but today it's used as an employee break room.

Then and Now: The Denver Mint once shared its block with homes and businesses. The alley and buildings, shown in this early photo, taken from atop the City and County Building across Cherokee Street, have been swallowed up by the Mint in its expansions. The entire block is now occupied by the Mint. (Photo Credit: Denver Public Library Western History Collection [historic photo] and R. Michael Field [contemporary photo])

Change in Quarters: Even before the 50 State Quarters Program™, the quarter saw changes. The Liberty Head (1892–1916), Standing Liberty (1916–1930), and Washington (1932–). (Photo Credit: R. Michael Field)

Gold! Ten-dollar gold eagle coins like these were melted into bullion after the 1934 Gold Reserve Act outlawed private ownership of gold coins, except for those with numismatic value. (Photo Credit: roundmetal, from Coin Page)

The gold was then transported to Denver by ordinary trains in horse-cars. Horse-cars were common and attracted little attention—even when packed with gold. Fifteen US marshals in civilian clothing accompanied each shipment. They moved two shipments each week, so only $10 million would be on the road at a time. As a shipment reached Denver, the next one left San Francisco. It took four months to get the job done, and the secrecy of the task was as closely guarded as the gold.[3]

Fast forward to the thirties. In 1934 Uncle Sam again selected Denver as the best location to store the country's gold. Two and one-half billion dollars in gold bullion—$36.4 billion by today's standard—moved 1,440 miles from San Francisco to Denver. The September 10, 1934, issue of *Time* magazine called it the greatest gold shipment of all time. This was one-third of all the gold in the country.[4] The country was rich with gold at this time because the Depression was easing. Colorado mines were also peaking in production.

Fort Knox was still being built, so Denver held more gold than had ever been collected in one place. According to the January 1, 1936, *Rocky Mountain News*, there was enough gold in the Denver Mint to gold leaf the entire surface of the world.

Unlike in 1908, however, this time the secret was out. Gold receipts and shipments were noted in local papers. Gold was shipped via US Mail in ordinary parcel post shipments or by train and was then transferred into mail trucks at the Denver depot. These were supposedly "secret" shipments, but convoys screamed through downtown, accompanied by police and guards. Newspapers speculated that the installation of floodlights at the rear of the Mint meant a $1.5 billion shipment of gold was on its way. Photographers showed up at the Union Pacific depot to snap

Gold Suitable for Storage: Gold bars stashed away for safekeeping. Bars of melted gold coins are more orange than the yellow certificate bars. (Photo Credit: U.S. Mint)

pictures. The public became accustomed to gold cargoes moving through the streets, like present-day residents of Washington, DC, who routinely wait for presidential motorcades. Undoubtedly, they became annoyed at the traffic delays caused when gold convoys passed.

Ironically, Denver was amassing gold just as President Franklin Roosevelt outlawed the possession of gold. The banking crisis in the United States reached a boiling point in 1933. Rumors of runaway inflation and ending the gold standard had created anarchy in American financial arenas. Banks were closing, and panicky gold owners were shipping their gold

Gold Lemon Bars

Crust:
2 cubes butter
½ cup sugar
2 cups flour
1/8 teaspoon salt

Filling:
4 eggs, lightly beaten
1¼ cups sugar
3 tablespoons flour
grated lemon zest from two large lemons
lemon juice from two large lemons (about 2/3 cup)
1/3 cup sweetened evaporated milk (regular milk can be substituted, if desired)
1/8 teaspoon salt
powdered sugar

Mix ingredients for crust in a mixer until crumbly. Mixture should resemble coarse meal. Press the mixture into a buttered 13-inch by 9-inch pan. Chill for 15 minutes, then bake at 350 degrees Fahrenheit for 20 minutes or until crust is just starting to brown.

As crust is baking, mix ingredients for filling. Whisk together eggs, sugar, and flour. Stir in lemon juice, lemon zest, milk, and salt. Blend well. When crust is removed from the oven, pour filling onto warm crust. Then bake for 20 to 25 minutes, or until filling is set. Filling should feel firm when touched lightly. Cool and sprinkle with powdered sugar. Good as gold!

offshore. To stop the bleeding of gold, Roosevelt closed the banks for four days and on January 30, 1934, passed the Gold Reserve Act, which required the public to return gold coins to the government in exchange for dollars. The only pieces exempt were those held solely for numismatic value. The price of gold increased to $35 an ounce from $20.67.

All those returned gold coins were eventually melted down into gold bullion. Some of it sits today in the Denver Mint in the form of gold bars. The average gold bar weighs about 27.5 pounds. At $500 an ounce, that equals $220,000, or nearly a quarter of a million dollars per bar. Dimensions are 7 inches by 3.625 inches by 1.75 inches, roughly the size of an ordinary building brick. Gold bars come in a large variety of shapes and sizes, depending on where they are made. Bars made at the Denver Mint have rounded corners and are stamped with identifying markings.

Visitors to the Mint are intrigued by the gold. Gold bars were displayed for Mint visitors until security was tightened after the Oklahoma City bombing in 1995. It was one of the most popular parts of the tour.

The gold at the Mint shows that this precious metal still has the power to entice, just as it did in ancient days. Coronado's golden cities were mythical, but the Denver Mint's gold is very real.

Chapter Notes

1. Frank Leach was the superintendent of the US Mint at San Francisco from 1897 to 1907 and director of the Mint at Washington, DC, from 1907 to 1909. He tells of transferring the gold from San Francisco to Denver in his book *Recollections of a Newspaper Man—A Record of Life and Events in California.*

2. David J. Eitemiller's book *The Denver Mint, The Story of the Mint from the Gold Rush to Today* has a description of the old sweeps cellar on page 39.

3. Records of gold transfers appeared regularly in area papers. A notice was also printed in the September 1934 issue *of The Numismatist* (which said Denver would be the largest gold depository of the time). Stories about gold and the vault appeared in the January 7, 1936, issue of the *Rocky Mountain News*, the February 3, 1938, edition of the *Denver Post* and the December 31, 1936, edition of the *Denver Post.*

4. We've tried to find out exactly how much gold is stored in the Denver Mint and gotten a variety of answers. The official word? According to the US Mint 2004 Annual Report, the US government inventory of gold contains 245,262,897 ounces—or nearly 8,000 tons—of gold. Guillermo Hernandez, public affairs director for the Denver Mint, told us the Mint has about one-fourth of the country's gold reserves.

CHAPTER FOUR

The Winds of War
(1940–1960)

B y the late 1930s, things were looking up in America. The Great Depression loosened its death grip on the country's jugular. Perhaps it was as the song promised; happy days were indeed here again. You could see it in the gold receipts at the Denver Mint.

Gold was pouring into the vaults—new gold, not the melted-down jewelry and coins the Mint had received in the early days of the Depression. This gold spilled from the mines of the West, as the industry ramped to unprecedented heights of production.

Demand for coins was up, signaling a better economy. People were spending money again. Newly implemented sales taxes added pennies to transactions, Social Security payroll deductions left odd amounts in paychecks, and the "coin in the slot" vending machines were becoming popular. Americans welcomed the novelty of dropping a coin into a machine that dispensed cold beverages, candy, and even sandwiches. Vending machines tied up coins for several days, but that was no problem. The Mint would simply make more.

Silver dollars, which had fallen so far out of fashion that the Mint had stopped producing them in 1934, were becoming popular again. Gambling, particularly around Army posts, fed the demand as soldiers used the "iron men" for poker chips. The Mint went into its reserve, issuing new silver dollars struck in the 1920s.

July 1940 found the Denver Mint running three shifts, seven days a week. By November the Mint could not keep up with the demand for coins for the first time since the end of World War I.

A second world war put the Denver Mint into the history books. In 1943, under the cloak of darkness, a plane landed at

Gold Vault Breached!

The *Rocky Mountain News* reported on June 1, 1945, the startling admission from Denver Mint Superintendent Moses E. Smith of a breach in the security protecting nearly half of America's gold reserves: "In 1937 we sealed up a vault containing $127 million worth of gold. We didn't know it at the time, but a grasshopper got in shortly before we sealed it up. When we opened the vault last year, there was that grasshopper, sitting on enough gold to buy out a millionaire's club."

One wonders if all that wealth changed the grasshopper? Did he forget his friends, his values, his very roots? Was he arrogantly perched atop the gold, draped in bling, sipping expensive champagne, and nibbling the finest caviar?

Superintendent Smith was less philosophical: "Boy, was he dead!"[1]

Lowry Field near Denver. Its shrouded cargo: 5 tons of gold spirited out of Russia, bound for the safety of the Denver Mint's impregnable vaults. The shipment, which arrived on the night of August 10 in three large Army planes, was the first ever received by air at the Denver Mint. Mint workers were called in from their homes that night to secure the gold in the vaults.[2]

Pennies Go to War

Like the rest of America, the Denver Mint jumped into the war effort. Both copper and nickel, the bulk materials for pennies and nickels, were on the strategic metals list, so the Mint had to change the "recipe" for its most popular coins.

Nickels made before 1943 were 75 percent copper and 25 percent nickel. Wartime nickels were 56 percent copper, 9 percent manganese, and 35 percent silver. Not only did the nickel contain no nickel, it was now more expensive to produce because of the added silver. It retained its pre-war looks, distinguished by a larger mintmark.

The penny also underwent radical change, losing its familiar copper shine. The 1943 penny was formulated of steel with a zinc coating. The penny's new look did not go over well with Americans, who complained that the silvery shine of zinc made the penny look too much like a dime. Depending on which side of the transaction you were on, that could be a bad thing. The Mint reworked the formula slightly, and the zinc coating darkened as the coins circulated, but the public never fully accepted the "white" pennies.

Virgin silver was in high demand. Over the years, worn

Good Housekeeping at the Mint

The Denver Post heralded Mint Superintendent Alva K. Schneider, the first of many women to hold that coveted position, with a banner headline praising the changes her feminine hand had wrought. "Good housekeeping has swept through the treasure and tradition-laden old institution like a broom," the newspaper crowed in 1954.

After the war the Denver Mint upgraded its operation dramatically, mechanizing processes such as palletizing coins so they could be moved with a forklift instead of human brawn. Although the newspaper acknowledged that Mrs. Schneider herself admitted to "a mechanical turn of mind," it called "traditional feminine love of order and efficiency" the key factor in the Mint's modernization.

Indeed, the Mint was more attractive on Mrs. Schneider's watch. She saw to it that the "tenement tan" walls received a fresh coat of "mint green" paint. She personally selected the perfect shade of sunny yellow for the cleaned-up lunchroom.

The accident rate at the coin factory plummeted and morale rose. Even President Eisenhower noticed. He commented on his tour, "Just goes to show that a woman can handle a big job like this if you give her a chance."

Mrs. Schneider called the presidential praise "a bouquet for womankind."

Now, That's a Marketing Gimmick! Automaker Pontiac gave out these money clips promoting their cars. Ironically, the money clip is designed to hold bills. America's preference for dollar bills is likely the main reason dollar coins do not circulate widely. (Photo Credit: R. Michael Field)

and mutilated silver dollar coins were taken out of circulation and stored in the vaults of the Mint. But by law no one, not even the Mint, could melt coins. It took an act of Congress in 1943 for the Mint to reclaim the silver in its hoards of retired silver dollars. Collectors clamored to buy the old coins, many from as far back as the Civil War, but the Mint was prohibited from selling coins that had been withdrawn from circulation. The hoard went into the melting pots. Numismatists across the country felt the flames of the furnace licking at their own hearts as the fires consumed the historic coins. The reclaimed silver was used to manufacture lesser coins, such as half-dollars, quarters, dimes, and the

Who Says You Can't Steal Coins From the Denver Mint?

Here's the first-hand account of a daring heist at the Denver Mint—straight from one of the "perps."

"It was 1954, maybe. I was in eighth grade, I think, when my class went on a field trip to the Denver Mint. There were all these nickels sitting in a bin, mistakes the Mint was going to melt down and reuse. A bunch of kids grabbed handfuls of the nickels.

"Of course, the Mint caught us. They gave us a stern lecture, and everyone had to empty their pockets. But I think some of those nickels made it out of there because kids were hiding them in their shoes and everywhere."

The sticky-fingered student—who will remain unidentified—thought his middle school (which will also remain unidentified) was banned from Mint tours for five years after the nickel-nicking incident.

Mint Supervisor Alma Schneider called an emergency meeting at the Mint which the children attended. "By the time we were through they were a sorry bunch, believe me," she told the *Rocky Mountain News*, adding that "the children of today don't seem to have the respect for government they used to have."[3]

Copper Penny Glazed Carrots

3 cups sliced carrots (sliced horizontally so they look like coins)
5 tablespoons butter
½ cup orange juice
½ cup honey
¼ teaspoon salt
¼ cup minced pecans

Steam carrots until tender-crisp (about 10 minutes). Drain, then put back into a medium saucepan. Add butter, orange juice, honey, and salt and cook, covered, over medium heat another 10-15 minutes, until tender.

newly formulated nickels.[4]

Rosie the Riveter Comes to the Mint

One wartime change at the Denver Mint was here to stay—women became part of the workforce. The American Numismatic Association (ANA) noted in its journal in April 1944 that when the "masculine money makers marched off to war," women served as punch machine operators and "manned" the reviewing tables, weighing machines, and counting and sacking machines. H. R. Hodgson, chief clerk of the San Francisco Mint, said, "Women are good workers, although they need help in heaving money bags." The female workers were investigated carefully by the Secret Service and hired for their "good character and honesty" just as their male counterparts were. Hodgson was quick to point out that "contrary to popular belief, there is nothing to the rumor that all mint workers are searched for coins as they go off duty."

The Denver Mint planned for these new female employees in its expansion of 1945. The ANA wrote in 1945, "In recent years, women in considerable numbers have gone to work in the Mint, performing operations that used to be considered suitable only for men. The new structure will have a special cafeteria and locker and toilet rooms for women." And yes, similar accommodations were provided for the men.[5]

Even before hostilities ceased, the Denver Mint prepared for a post-war that would be anything but peaceful. The first order of business was making coins for foreign governments. In 1945 nearly half of the Denver Mint's capacity was devoted to coining for countries devastated by war and for newly emerging countries. Many of the coins were exotic, such as the silver and copper pieces minted for the Dutch East Indies. Those coins had a hole punched through their centers so people could wear them around their necks until they were ready to spend them. Foreign customers included the Philippines, Liberia, Panama, Mexico, the Netherlands, and even China. By the war's end, the Denver Mint turned out more coins than all three US mints did in 1937, before wartime demand kicked up production. All while making

The War Prize

During World War II, the Mint's presses cranked out billions of coins. While production soared, mistakes were made. But hey, a war was on.

To save precious copper, the 1943 penny was reformulated to zinc-coated steel. *Except for those few that were struck onto copper blanks!*

Because the "white" coins were much maligned, the Mint shifted gears and in 1944 struck pennies from salvaged shell casings. The brass alloy looks virtually the same as the pre-war pennies. Once again, shiny coppery pennies rolled off the presses. *Except for those few that were struck onto steel blanks!*

Instant collectibles were born, as well as instant fakes. Copper-plated 1943 and zinc-coated 1944 pennies appeared almost immediately. Hint: A real 1943 steel cent will stick to a magnet whereas a copper coin will not.

So, check your change. A copper 1943 or a steel 1944 cent is worth a pretty penny!

The Denver Mint's Main Entry: During the 1940s and 1950s, visitors passed through massive doors at the Denver Mint's main entrance on West Colfax Avenue. Except for the addition of the iron fence, it is virtually unchanged since the Mint's opening. (Photo Credit: R. Michael Field)

The Visitor's Entrance: Public tours begin in this 1980s addition to the Mint. Its plain, stark design caused consternation among historic preservationists. Government construction budgets, however, had little room for buildings inspired by Medici palaces. While nothing can imitate granite, advances in architectural pre-cast concrete panels allow the Mint to complement the graceful arches and textures of the early structure. (Photo Credit: David Hall)

Decades of Dimes: The dime as it evolved over the 20th century. The Barber dime (1892–1916), the Mercury Head or Winged Liberty (1916–1945) and the Roosevelt dime (1946–) (Photo Credit: R. Michael Field)

millions of foreign coins.

Remember all the copper that *didn't* go into pennies during the war? It was back—in the form of brass shell casings. The 50-caliber machine gun was *the* heavy machine gun of World War II. Whether on aircraft, ships, or tanks, it inflicted a lot of damage on the enemy and saved countless American lives. After the war, millions upon millions of the 4-inch brass cartridge cases arrived at the Denver Mint to begin their peacetime lives as pennies.

Soon 15 tons of casings a month were shoveled into Denver's furnaces. The copper was used to make 30 million pennies each month. The Mint ceased production of the much-maligned steel penny, but the coin remained in circulation.

Flush But Frightened

The nation reveled in a post-war boom but soon faced another war—the Cold War. Denverites opened their newspapers to learn that the Soviet Union possessed the atom bomb. Communism swept the world as the Balkan states, a partitioned Germany, and China fell in its wake. And on the Korean peninsula, war broke out once more.

Americans were working, buying homes, and having babies in unprecedented numbers. But there was a shadow of atomic annihilation over the 1950s. The nation enjoyed wealth, but it craved security.

Security was put on display at the Denver Mint. Denver newspapers in the early 1950s chronicled the intimidating measures the Mint took to protect all that money. Bulletproof doors and great gates of steel suitably impressed a public that wanted clear signs that the Mint was serious about protecting the nation's gold assets. Mint Superintendent Alma K. Schneider proudly showed off the state-of-the-art technical innovations of Mint security to a *Rocky Mountain*

News columnist during a 1953 tour, patting the marble wall as she described the vibration-sensitive alarms and pointing out tear gas jets that could flood the building with a debilitating chemical mist.

Newspapers assured readers that the Mint police were ever vigilant in protecting the coin factory. In a 1950 *Denver Post* photo, the guard at the front door made no effort to hide his Thompson submachine gun. A 1953 *Rocky Mountain News* account of a visit to the Mint described how the guard suspiciously eyed the reporter from the machine gun nest that still hangs from the staircase in the lobby. Sharpshooters of the Mint police practiced daily at the gunnery range in the basement to maintain their status as crack shots. (Incidentally, they still do.)

It's hard to imagine the facility standing unprotected amid lush, inviting lawns, but a fence was not added until 1955. The sturdy fence of tall iron spikes was secondary to the alarms and firepower inside the coin fortress, but it added a significant level of protection while presenting the look of safety and security to the public.[6]

New Challenges for a New World

Americans settled into post-war boom of the 1950s. However, the Mint would have no time to enjoy the peace because every family photograph taken would make minting coins more difficult. The reason? Silver! Photography used silver, and Americans had discovered how to take snapshots. The end of the 1950s locked the Mint in competition not only with the family Brownie camera, but also with a brand-new, silver-consuming industry—the space program.

Demand for silver was soaring. From 1950 to 1965 industrial and arts usage of silver rose an average of 4 percent a year while supply grew only 1.5 percent. In just two years, "free silver," the Treasury supply not used as backing for silver certificates, plummeted by 90 percent.

The magic number was "$1.30." A silver dollar contained .77 ounce of silver. When silver reached $1.30 per ounce, it began to pay to start melting silver dollars. Minor circulating coins were close behind at a $1.38 per ounce price for silver. The 1950s closed as speculators stockpiled silver and the Mint scrambled for a solution to the coming crisis. [7]

Chapter Notes

1. Superintendent Moses E. Smith always spoke proudly of the Denver Mint, and he told great stories. His tale of the grasshopper in the gold vault appeared in the June 1, 1945, issue of the *Rocky Mountain News*.

2. The story about Russian gold appeared in the *Denver Post* on January 3, 1943. Indeed, the vaults of the United States held many treasures during World War II, including Britain's Magna Carta, which was stored at Fort Knox.

3. When we were researching and writing this book, we asked everyone we knew, even perfect strangers, if they knew of anyone who had worked at the Denver Mint, had a story about the Denver Mint, or had robbed the Denver Mint—the latter of which always brought a few chuckles. It paid off, though, when a friend of a friend shared his delightful story of a childhood prank we call the Nickel Nicking Incident.

    The *Rocky Mountain News* reported the story on March 27, 1954. In the news account by David Stolberg, the stolen coins were described as blanks, not nickels. Because the blanks were of the correct size and had their rims raised, they worked in vending machines, so the youngsters used them. In their minds, they were nickels!

    Our unnamed perpetrator recalled the incident vividly, even after more than 50 years.

4. Alfred J. Swails covers war pennies and changing formulae for coins during World War II extensively in *World War II Remembered*, a numismatic journal. Mint statistics and formulae for the composition of coins were reported in the *Rocky Mountain News* throughout the 1940s.

5. It's tough to find information about the Denver Mint's workforce during World War II, but the librarians at the

ANA Money Museum in Colorado Springs steered us to articles in the *ANA Journal*. Specifically, we referenced the April 1944 (volume 57, page 317) and October 1945 (volume 58, page 1098) issues.

6. Security measures were detailed in articles in the *Denver Post* in the 1950s. *Denver Post* staff writer Edith Eudora Kohl reported on her visit to the gold vaults of the Denver Mint in the *Denver Post* on November 26, 1950. Other articles were quite humorous, such as "Mint Controlled by Tightwads" by Robert "One for the Money" Stapp in the *Rocky Mountain News* on September 6, 1953.

7. Statistics and information about the silver shortage in the 1950s is from Ginger Rapsus's book *The United States Clad Coinage*.

CHAPTER FIVE

Scantily Clad Coins (1960–1970)

The sixties blasted through the United States like a tidal wave. Everything changed—hairstyles, skirt lengths, sexual norms. In the scope of things, it's easy to forget that money changed, too. But it did. While the hippies were trying to reform the world through rock music, drugs, and free love, the Mint had its own transformation, in the form of a new kind of coin—the sandwich coin (or "clad coin," in numismatic terminology). Silver was out; copper and nickel were in.

You'd think we'd barely notice. But we did. And at first Americans weren't crazy about those new coins. So why did the Mint introduce them?

The Mint didn't alter the nation's coins just for fun. Nor were they concerned about staying in style with the changing times. The introduction of clad coins wasn't even something the Mint necessarily *wanted* to do. They *needed* to do it or the country would run out of silver.

Prior to 1965 silver was used to make quarters, dimes, half-dollars, and dollar coins. During the early sixties, however, the country's silver supply was in crisis. The country was quickly outgrowing its silver supply, and the price of silver was steadily climbing. Industries, especially those related to space, the arts, and photography, were using increasing amounts of silver. The US Treasury gave silver to industry in return for silver certificates. This increased the demand for silver even more. People began to hoard silver, and the price was rising so fast it was almost worth it to melt down coins simply for the price of the silver.

At the time, coins were 90 percent silver and 10 percent copper. And like the silver they were made from, coins were in short supply.

Who Didn't *Hoard* Silver? *Americans knew the silver coins were worth saving. They tucked them away in tin cans, old milk bottles and probably inside a few mattresses. These were buried in a coffee can by author Kimberly Field's parents! (Photo Credit: R. Michael Field)*

The sixties coin shortage was unprecedented. The scarcity wasn't merely in the minds of economists and coin dealers. It was a daily reality for Americans. Signs requesting exact change were posted in stores. Gamblers paid more than face value for coins to use in slot machines. A few companies resorted to printing certificates to be used in place of coins and redeeming wooden nickels. These emergency measures violated laws and were quickly shut down.

Like a perfect storm in the Atlantic, a confluence of specific events spun the problem out of control. The coin shortage was unique because it didn't result from financial panic or war. The silver crisis was a major factor. Also, usage of vending machines had increased. Coins were frequently left inside pay phones, parking meters, and other vending machines for up to a month, keeping them out of general circulation.

Beyond vending machines, though, were the demands of daily commerce. The baby boom had hit the country with a vengeance. Obviously, more people needed more money. Coin reserves could not keep up with the demands of the expanding population.

To make matters worse, the San Francisco Mint had recently closed, leaving the Denver Mint and Philadelphia Mint to make all the coins. The Denver Mint was making 60 percent of the coins. Employees at both mints were working twenty-four hours a day, seven days a week, and the mints had ordered new equipment to make more coins.

The assassination of John F. Kennedy in 1963 also played a part in the coin shortage. People saved Kennedy half dollars, which were introduced in March 1964, to memorialize President Kennedy. Noncollectors and even foreigners wanted Kennedy half-dollars.

Treasury officials put partial blame for the dearth of coins on collectors. Indeed, coin collecting was popular. By mid-

1964 more than 8 million people actively collected mint sets. Courses in coin investing ran at universities. Major department stores had coin departments. Treasury officials claimed collectors kept coins out of circulation by hoarding, amassing complete sets of annual coins, and stockpiling coins for speculative purposes. A bill was eventually introduced that made coin collecting illegal. (Mild-mannered coin collectors as criminals—imagine that!) That bill did not pass, but the Treasury Department discouraged coin collecting in June 1964 by requesting that all coins continue to carry the 1964 date, even past the end of that year. They knew that date-frozen coins would be less attractive to collectors and hoarders.

A Solid Foundation for Any Coin Collection

Two popular products among coin collectors are uncirculated and proof annual coin sets. The Denver and Philadelphia Mints produce uncirculated annual coin sets. The mints strike these sets on polished blanks with carefully-inspected dies to ensure a crisp, clear strike.

The US Mint first produced uncirculated coin sets for collectors in 1947. They've been offered each year (except in 1950) in higher and higher numbers to meet collector demand. Now collectors scoop up millions of sets each year. Uncirculated coins show no evidence of use; however, they can display blemishes such as bag marks, contact marks, or lack of luster. Values of uncirculated coin sets vary by the condition of the coins. We found uncirculated coin sets on eBay, ranging from five times the original purchase price to nearly 15 percent under original price.

Proof sets are artistic renderings of coins in each denomination struck in a given year. The high-relief, sculpted foreground stands in sharp contrast to mirror-like backgrounds,

(continued on next page)

Understandably, coin collectors felt like scapegoats. Collectors shot off letters of protest to magazines and members of Congress. Their outcry was not successful. On September 3, 1964, President Lyndon B. Johnson authorized the date freeze. Mintmarks were also removed from coins, again to narrow the variety of coins that were collected. A date freeze, however, was not enough to solve the coin crunch. After much research and discussion, one thing was clear: If the United States continued to use silver in coinage, the supplies would be depleted within about three years.

The Coinage Act of 1965 authorized a major change. Silver would be eliminated from the dime and quarter and reduced in the half-dollar. Battelle, a science and technology

giving the coins a "cameo" appearance. Produced at the US Mint in San Francisco, proofs are made using specially polished blanks. The Mint strikes these burnished blanks with hand-polished dies two or more times on calibrated presses so every detail is sharp and in high relief. Proof sets are minted in silver as well as clad varieties. While they are legal tender, they command a premium because of their special treatment and packaging. A five-coin proof set of the state quarters that were minted in 2006 sells for $15.95 at the Denver Mint.

There are many "collectibles" on the market—from replica coins to colored coins to holographic renderings. But these are not made by the US Mint; they are not US legal tender. Manufacturers often will make the coins much larger (called giant proofs) and change surface details to avoid copyright infringement. A good information source on genuine US Mint collectibles and timely information on unauthorized products may be found on the US Mint's Web site at usmint.gov/consumer/index.cfm?action=consumer.

Coin collecting is like any other form of collecting. Learn from a reliable source, such as a reputable dealer, the American Numismatic Association, or the US Mint itself. And collect what has meaning to you.

Mintmarks

Every coin made at the Denver Mint carries a mintmark— the tiny letter D that shows the coin comes from Denver. Other mints also use them—an S for San Francisco, a P for Philadelphia, and a W for West Point. The practice is an old one. Coins from ancient Rome and Greece have mintmarks, as do coins from foreign countries. Mintmarks are used to identify where a specific coin is made.

Mintmarks for US coins began in 1835, when branch mints were first established. Mintmarks ensured that coinage from different branches was standardized. They also gave individual mints accountability for the coins they produced.

Coins from the Denver Mint have always carried mintmarks. The only time they haven't been used is when they were frozen during the coin shortage of the sixties to discourage coin investments. Mintmarks did not appear on coins from the Denver Mint during 1965, 1966, and 1967.

Mintmarks on US coins are not intended to be decorative. Their purpose is simply for identification, and thus they are inconspicuous.

Mint Marks on US Coinage Through the Years:
C = Charlotte, North Carolina
CC = Carson City, Nevada
D = Denver, Colorado
O = New Orleans, Louisiana
P = Philadelphia, Pennsylvania
S = San Francisco, California
W = West Point Mint (West Point makes gold and silver commemorative coins for collectors. Pennies were minted at West Point from 1973 to 1986, but these coins bore no mintmark.)
No mark = Philadelphia, Pennsylvania (At first, coins minted in Philadelphia did not need a mintmark since it was the country's only mint. The "P" mintmark still does not appear on pennies.)
D = Dahlonega, Georgia (1838 to 1861 Gold)

Coils Awaiting Their New Lives as Coins: The Denver Mint began buying sheets of alloyed metal to produce sandwich coins. Metal coils weighing up to 6,000 pounds sit on the south dock. The coils, if unrolled, would stretch for a quarter mile. (Photo Credit: R. Michael Field)

The 1964 Peace Dollar—What Were They Thinking?

In 1964 the country was running out of silver at an alarming rate. Silver prices were skyrocketing. People were hoarding silver coins, and speculators were hanging onto bags of silver coins, hoping silver prices would get so high the coins would literally be worth their weight in, uh, silver. There couldn't have been a worse time to mint a silver dollar. But that's what the boys in Washington decided to do.

What were they thinking?

The 1964 peace dollar was perhaps the most ill-conceived idea in the history of American money. This folly created a coin that could be worth a lot of money for coin collectors—that is, if one actually exists.

There is some question about that. The story of the '64 Peace Dollar is shrouded in mystery even to this day. Let's go back a few decades and see what the fuss was all about.

The '64 Peace Dollar was the brainchild of President Lyndon B. Johnson's administration. Western legislators encouraged the idea, stating that silver dollars were an important part of the West and that mining in western states would benefit from the minting of silver dollars.

Treasury officials balked, as did many members of Congress. Coin experts were baffled. Tom Wass, the president of International Numismatics Corporation, said, "Everyone's crying about the silver shortage, and now the government's throwing away $45 million on silver dollars nobody needs."[1]

Johnson and the Western senators prevailed. On May 15, 1965, President Johnson issued an order to begin production. The same design was used as the original Peace Dollars that were minted after World War I. The obverse depicted a profile of Miss Liberty with a crown of rays, while the reverse showed an eagle perched on a rock, clasping in its talons a laurel wreath

(continued on next page)

representing peace. So far, so good, right?

The Denver Mint struck 316,076 of these dollars. But Congress continued to denounce the plan. With good reason. The price for the dollars rapidly became inflated among coin dealers—up to $7.50 per piece—and ripe for hoarding. After only ten days of production, Washington ordered the Mint to stop making the coins. Existing coins were to be melted. The Mint complied with the request.

So what's the problem? Dollars made; dollars melted. It's official—no '64 Peace Dollars.

But what if a few survived? Speculation abounds that a few coins made it out of the Mint, despite claims to the contrary from the Mint and Treasury Department. In 1972 a report appeared in a commodities newsletter that some coins had made it into the hands of private dealers. Is it merely coincidence that this report appeared when the statute of limitations had expired for prosecution for someone who removed these coins from the Mint?

In 1973 a coin dealer placed an ad in the official journal of the American Numismatic Association offering $3,000 for the coin. Tentative offers and inquiries were made, but no coins were produced. Then the government issued a press release stating that the coins were illegal since they were officially still the property of the US government and therefore would be confiscated. If the coins had existed, their owners were undoubtedly scared away.

Since that time, no coins have turned up, although rumors continue to fester. If a '64 Peace Dollar exists, it likely will stay tucked away in a collector's home or may turn up eventually in a foreign country. That's too bad. The '64 Peace Dollar was the end of the silver coin era in the United States. We may never know what the politicians were thinking, but odds are they'll never mint silver dollars again. [2]

Half-Dollars over the Years: In the 20th century, Walking Liberty (1916–1947), Benjamin Franklin (1948–1963), and President John F. Kennedy (1964–) graced half-dollar coins. (Photo Credit: R. Michael Field)

firm, conducted a study about the metallurgical feasibility for new coinage. The result? Sandwich coins. A copper core would be "sandwiched" between outer layers of a nickel alloy. The Treasury Department distributed an eight-page brochure about the coins, and the June 11, 1965, issue of *Time* magazine tried to make the coins sound exotic: "The US will have the world's only two-colored coins." But the public had other ideas when the clads were released in November 1965.

Clad coins ushered in a new era of money in the United States. Up until that point, coins had intrinsic value. They were originally issued with the idea that every coin's face value was equal to its real value. Clad coins, however, had no intrinsic value.

To find out how people felt about the sandwich coins, ask anyone who was around when they came out. They will probably tell you they didn't like them. They might voice their suspicion that the government was trying to cheat them. They'd probably say that money was worth less or that the new coins looked strange.

A few people disliked the new coins so much they wouldn't accept them in change. Even some businesses got into the act, offering goods at discounted prices for customers who paid in silver coins. Not surprisingly, folks started to stash their silver coins away, and within a few years it was nearly impossible to find silver coins in circulation. Meanwhile, white-haired grandfathers and middle-aged housewives had old mayonnaise jars or tin cans full of them sitting in their pantries or bedroom closets.

Collectors didn't welcome the dawn of clad coinage, either. They bemoaned the quality of the new coins ("Ugly! Worthless!") and weren't happy with the detail of the coins, the feel of the metal, and the "thunking" sound they made when dropped. The Mint cranked out the clads in enormous numbers, yet another reason for collectors to

The Kennedy Half-Dollar: Since the Franklin half dollar had not been in circulation for 25 years, it took an act of Congress to authorize the Kennedy half-dollar. The Kennedy inaugural medal served as a model for the profile head of the slain President on the new coin. Mrs. Kennedy played an active role in approving the concepts. The silver coin minted after President John F. Kennedy's assassination, was snapped up by avid collectors and silver-hoarders. (Photo Credit: R. Michael Field)

shun them.[3]

Despite the chilly reception, the coins circulated widely. We Americans are a forgiving type, and we need our coins. So we spent them and learned that they spent the same as the silver coins. Date marks returned in 1967 and mintmarks returned in 1968. The coin shortage ended.

Collectors continued to reject the sandwich coins. But in recent years, even that has changed as collectors have begun to find clads more desirable. The fact is, clads are here to stay. It's more likely that Elvis Presley will be

Denver Mint Brownies
(Courtesy of Collin and Danae Sloan, from an old family recipe)

Brownie layer:
21½ -ounce fudge brownie mix
½ cup water
½ cup vegetable oil
1 egg
½ teaspoon mint extract, if desired

Mint filling:
½ cup butter
3 ounces cream cheese, softened
2½ cups powdered sugar
3 tablespoons crème de mint syrup

Frosting:
6 ounces semisweet chocolate chips
1/3 cup margarine

In a large bowl, mix brownie layer with water, vegetable oil, egg, and mint extract. Bake in a greased 9-inch by 13-inch pan, according to package directions (approximately 24 minutes—don't over bake). Cool completely.

In a medium bowl, combine butter and cream cheese. Beat until light and fluffy. Add powdered sugar and crème de mint syrup and beat until smooth. Spread over brownie layer and cool in refrigerator.

In a small saucepan, melt chocolate chips and margarine on low heat until smooth, stirring constantly. Remove from heat and cool for 15 minutes. Spread to cover filling. Cool in refrigerator before cutting.

Sweeps Cellar

Sweeps Cellar Gets a New Life: The sweeps cellar, in which metal debris was stored, was no longer needed when the Denver Mint stopped casting its own ingots. Now, it houses an employee break room. (Photo Credit: R. Michael Field)

discovered alive in Boise, Idaho, than that the United States will return to silver coins.

The story of the clad coins tells us something about how we *feel* about our money. We like to think coins are just insignificant pieces of metal that roll around in our wallets until we want to buy a Snickers bar from a vending machine. But maybe it's not such a casual relationship. We like certain coins, love some, and completely reject others. Nothing showed that more than the biggest failure in coin history, which was to come in the seventies—the Susan B. Anthony dollar. Compared to the Suzy Bs, clad coins were superstars.

Chapter Notes

1. We used an excellent, comprehensive book about the history of clad coins and the '64 Peace Dollar to research this time in the Mint's history: *The United States Clad Coinage* by Ginger Rapsus. The quote from Tom Wass can be found on page 10.

2. The Web site of Professional Coin Grading Service has also shed light on these topics (www.pcgs.com).

3. We have spoken to everyone we know who's old enough to remember the dawn of sandwich coins in America. We were amazed by the strong feelings on this topic, the rich memories, and the similarity of experiences. We're still waiting to find the person who actually turned in their silver coins.

CHAPTER SIX

Decades of Dubious Developments (1970–1990)

If you head to your local 7-Eleven and buy a Coke with a dollar coin, the clerk is likely to gape at the coin, look at you askance, then pose the question, "What is this?" Even though dollar coins have been minted since 1794—and millions of dollars have rolled off the machines at the Denver Mint—you may never have seen one.

The Tale of the Susan B. Anthony Dollar—Proving Once and for All That Size Matters

The Europeans love their Euro coins, Canadians their gold- and silver-toned loonies, the British the thick, chunky pound. We Americans stick to our paper dollars. Our experience with dollar coins in the last thirty years does not show evidence of changing this trend.

In the mid-seventies, the Carter administration proposed the idea of a new dollar coin. The last time Americans had seen dollar coins was in 1971, when the Eisenhower dollar coin was struck. It was a large silver coin honoring the first landing on the moon, but it failed to circulate widely. The public wasn't crazy about its unwieldy size. Still, people needed dollar coins, mostly for gambling and vending machines.

Well, we Americans are a persistent bunch. The moneymakers in the seventies certainly were. Why let the failure of a big, clunky coin deprive the American people of a workable dollar coin? The US Mint assigned the Research Triangle Institute to study the matter, and the recommendation was clear: Give Americans a smaller dollar coin.

Concern for the fate of gamblers was not the primary consideration in this decision. Money was. Flimsy paper

The Realistic, Non-allegorical (and some say non-beautiful) Susan B. Anthony Dollar: The depiction of the suffragette was not considered attractive. (Photo Credit: U.S. Mint)

dollars last only eighteen months, compared to coins that can last for ten to fifteen years. Millions of dollars could be saved if some of our paper money could be replaced by a sturdy dollar coin. Hence, the concept of a mini-dollar coin was launched.

The next decision? Who to put on the dollar. Until this point coins were engraved with the faces of presidents and eagles, liberty bells and laurel wreaths, and various images of a symbolic woman representing liberty. A portrait of a real woman had never been on a coin.

The seventies were the perfect time to change this precedent. Bras were still charred from the women's liberation movement and feminism flourished. Women's groups were hammering out the thorny issue of equal pay for equal work, abortion had just become legal, and women's studies programs were being created in dozens of universities.

Despite the atmosphere of the country, the Treasury Department favored yet another allegorical Miss Liberty with flowing hair and noble features. Then Mary Rose Oakar, representative from Ohio, introduced a bill suggesting that a portrait of Susan B. Anthony, the famed women's suffragist, appear on the new dollar coin.

Not surprisingly, the suggestion inflamed some members of Congress, along with some collectors. The debate raged in Congress, while various women's groups came out in favor of the Anthony design. Colorado Congresswoman Patricia Schroeder argued, "We have had live eagles and live buffaloes on our coins, but never have we had a live woman." Eventually Oakar's bill won favor, and Susan B. Anthony was chosen to appear on the coin.

So it was that 757,813,744 shiny Susan B. Anthony dollars made their debut in 1979. The clunk was so loud it could have shattered eardrums from New York to Los Angeles.

The Changing Face of Allegorical Beauty: Over the years, Liberty as depicted on the dollar coin has changed, reflecting the tastes of the era.

In 1795, Liberty's hair is loose and flowing. (Photo Credit: roundmetal, from Coin Page)

A century later, she sports a fussy Victorian hairdo on the Morgan dollar. (Photo Credit: greattoning, from Coin Page)

Though minted in the 1920s, Liberty on the Peace Dollar did not bob her hair. Instead, she looks perhaps her loveliest. (Photo Credit: roundmetal, from Coin Page)

People hated the dollars. Nicknames for them sprouted like dandelions. *Susan B. Agonies. Carter Quarters* and *JC Pennies*, in a nod to Jimmy Carter. They were far too similar to quarters, both in their silver color and size. The diameter of the two coins varied by about 2 millimeters. The Mint had set out to make a smaller dollar coin, and they had certainly done that. But they'd gone too far. The coin was too small.

The coins didn't fit into vending machines. Cash register drawers didn't have a space for them. Stores didn't want to use them, and some refused to accept them. One thing was clear: When it came to money, size mattered.

Size wasn't the only problem. Some felt that the small dollars perfectly represented the economy—a period of double-digit inflation, an energy crisis, and a shrinking dollar. People also thought the coins were ugly. They felt Susan B. Anthony's image was too stern and—let's just call it as it was—too homely to be on a coin.

Anthony's appearance was a

Silver Dollar Pancakes

1¼ cups all-purpose flour
1 large egg
1½ cups buttermilk
3 to 4 tablespoons sugar (to taste)
1 teaspoon baking power
1 teaspoon baking soda
¼ cup oil (canola, vegetable, or corn oil)

While mixing ingredients, preheat a skillet or griddle over medium heat. Spray with nonstick cooking spray or add a tablespoon of oil. In a mixer, combine all the above ingredients. Mix until smooth. Don't overdo it; it's okay if there are a few lumps. Ladle a small amount onto hot skillet, in the size of silver dollars (round circles about 1½ to 2 inches in diameter). When the top bubbles and the edges look hard, flip. When they're golden brown, they're done. Watch carefully—silver dollar pancakes cook fast!
Makes 30 to 40 silver dollar pancakes.

question earlier in the design process. Chief Mint Engraver Frank Gasparro designed the coin (the Flowing Hair Miss Liberty as well as Susan B. Anthony's portrait), and the Commission of Fine Arts was not pleased with his first design.[1] It "...wanted less glamour, more toughness, less refinement, and more of Anthony's real strong face." One has to wonder whether there was ever such a fuss over Jefferson's somber profile on the quarter or Washington's unsmiling face on the dollar bill. Nonetheless, Gasparro redid the design, making Anthony more severe. The verdict from the American public was unequivocal: The coin was ugly, the portrait unattractive.

Banks didn't order the sparkling new dollars, and consumers shunned them. They piled up in Federal Reserve banks and sat there, forgotten and unwanted.[2]

The statistics tell us everything we need to know: $800 million were struck at all three US mints in 1979. The next year, the mints produced a trifling 42 million. By May 1980 production stopped entirely, and in 1981 the only Suzies struck were for collectors. The supply of Susan B. Anthony dollars didn't dwindle until well into the nineties.

The good news is that yesterday's ho-hum Suzy Bucks are beginning to attract today's collectors. They are easy to get, their value is rising, and their checkered past is an intriguing side note. Who knows, maybe Susan B. Anthony may get the last laugh.[3]

Over My Dead Body

In 1966, sixty years after the Mint began coinage, Denver again felt hot embarrassment flush its cheeks when it cast an eye toward the Mint's physical structure. The roof leaked, ventilation was bad, and crowded conditions dictated that spacious hallways be carved up into offices. The Mint's presses generated such a racket that a judge across the street in the City and County Building complained that he couldn't hold court. Local wags sneered at its "pedestrian" architecture and complained about the eyesore of the south storage yard, jammed with cartons stacked like the supply dump of a factory. An ugly chain link fence did nothing to screen the unpleasant sight. At least no one accused the Mint of stinking up the neighborhood, like the Victorian Denverites had.

By the mid-1960s, there had been no fewer than twenty-one bills introduced in Congress to relocate Denver's Mint. It may have needed a facelift, but the Mint would still provide high-paying jobs and tourism revenue.

Denver Mayor Bill McNichols championed keeping the Mint in his city, saying that he enjoyed hearing the clinking of money there. It's more likely that he appreciated the tax revenue piling into city coffers. In the late 1960s, the Denver Mint's annual payroll totaled $2 million, with another $500,000 in supply purchases—that's $12 million by today's dollars.

In 1967 a new Mint facility was finished in Philadelphia. It set the standard for modern coining operations. Despite its shortcomings, the ugly duckling Denver Mint produced 70 to 75 percent of the nation's coinage, while maintaining a smaller work force than the belle of the coinage ball, the Philadelphia Mint.

That year New York architectural firm Parson-Jurden, commissioned by the Treasury Department to make recommendations for the Denver Mint facility, presented the case to keep the Mint in Denver—with major modernizing. Their study offered five plans to bring the Denver Mint up to the new standards; four of the five plans suggested renovating the current structure, including demolishing the exterior walls. One plan proposed the acquisition of adjacent property (a strategy employed in Mint expansion for decades), but the price of downtown real estate was an exorbitant $12 a square foot, leading some Denverites to wonder why you would put a manufacturing facility on prime urban space.

The deal breaker for renovation was not the destruction of the beautiful granite exterior of a bygone era. It was the loss of onsite parking. Parking wouldn't be a problem at the sprawling Federal Center just west of Denver in Jefferson County. Parson-Jurden suggested building a new Mint, from the ground up, on land already owned by the federal government. The Federal Center was roomy, with plenty of land for future expansions, and was well situated near a major highway. But it was not Denver.

A Mint to Match Our City

Like the Mint, Denver was a bit down on its heels by 1970. The downtown was decaying and jobs were fleeing the core city to the suburbs, as in many American cities at the time. Led by Mayor McNichols and Congresswoman Patricia Schroeder, a Democrat representing the urban First District, Denver resolved to keep its Mint.

Even the US Mint in Washington expressed a desire to keep the operation in Denver. The dream site for a new facility, according to the Mint, was 10 to 15 acres in Denver near a railroad spur, convenient to tourists.

It didn't take a divining rod to find the dream site in the Platte River Valley. Perfection lay along the West Bank of the South Platte River at Interstate 25 and Speer Boulevard. It sat just east of Mile High Stadium where the Denver Broncos played football and west of the railroad tracks. Best of all, it was in Denver city limits.

The Burlington and Northern Railroad, owners of the property, also thought it was a dream site—for the railroad, *not* the Denver Mint. Despite a full-court press from the city, the railroad refused to relinquish its right of way. Denver was back to square one as eyes once again turned to the Federal Center in the land known as "Not Denver."

Off Come the Gloves

Denver opened several fronts in its war to keep the Mint. In 1972 City Council set aside nearly $3 million to acquire a site that could then be sold to the federal government at a greatly reduced rate to offset the benefits of building at the Federal Center. Soon more drastic steps were needed, and in 1974 Denver played the "Mint at Denver" card. Pointing to sections 261 and 262 of the US Code, city attorneys argued that the 1895 Congressional Act establishing the Mint specifically called for a "Mint at Denver." Not a "Mint at unincorporated Jefferson County" or anywhere else. The federal government never fully bought that argument, but its attention was quickly diverted by Denver's presentation of an alternative site: the Park Hill Golf Course.

The Park Hill Golf Course sat on 35 acres of land at Colorado Boulevard and Smith Road within an integrated residential area. The city took its $2.9 million war chest and bought a chunk of the land. As part of the deal, Denver relocated nine holes to another part of the property. The site was then sold (at a deeply discounted rate) to the federal government, and plans began for the new Denver Mint.[4]

Then the folks from Gates Rubber Company called. The company had a 425,000-square-foot manufacturing plant less than five years old in Littleton. It had never been used to make tires, but it was perfect for manufacturing coins.

Aside from simply being "not Denver," Littleton represented the worst nightmare of those who feared flight

Littleton Site That Was Almost the Denver Mint: This former tire factory was considered a suitable site for the Denver Mint mostly because of cost considerations. In hindsight, it seems a poor choice. In the 1970s when the Mint considered moving here, Littleton was a fiercely independent town with farming and ranching roots. Aerospace, oil exploration and engineering firms were moving into Littleton. It had never been a manufacturing center and was far from the neighborhoods that traditionally had supplied Denver's manufacturing workforce. At the time, public transportation from Denver to the southern reaches of Arapahoe County was spotty. Many of the roads that are now Littleton thoroughfares were dirt! Indeed, for some of those reasons, the Gates Rubber Company abandoned its plans to move its own manufacturing to the facility the company had built.

Today, the facility lies on Mineral Road, a major east-west corridor through Littleton. Its neighborhood is primarily residential. Long-term tenants of the facility have included a major defense contractor and telecommunications company. (Photo Credit: R. Michael Field)

from the core city. The factory was *beyond* the suburbs, far south in Arapahoe County. Any tourists that would make the nearly 20-mile trip from downtown Denver could have spied antelope grazing on the prairie and maybe spotted a coyote hunting amid Yucca plants and cactus. The views of the mountains and plains were unmatched, and from the site you could glimpse the Denver skyline. The site seemed overwhelmingly cost-effective, with estimates that it would be nearly half as costly to convert the plant as to build in Park Hill.

Congresswoman Schroeder lashed out at her colleague Bill Armstrong, a Republican representing the Fifth District. Decrying the eleventh-hour proposal as political chicanery to deliver the Mint to his district just in time for the election, Schroeder accused Republicans of not caring about cities like Denver. Armstrong maintained that he simply liked the numbers—as did the US Treasury.

The City of Littleton was lukewarm about having the Mint in its midst. Acquisition by the government would take a prime manufacturing location off the city tax rolls, and the city wasn't sure the resulting jobs would offset that loss. Mint employees also had mixed feelings about both the Park Hill and Littleton sites. Either would result in long commutes. [5]

McNichols, Schroeder, and others geared up to fight the battle they thought they had won. Hadn't the federal government already purchased the Park Hill site? Schroeder demanded and received additional feasibility studies that she hoped would narrow the economic gap between the Park Hill site and the interloper from the south.

As the battle raged, Washington concluded that a new Mint was not necessary. The Vietnam conflict had drained the country's finances, and the country was settling into what President Jimmy Carter would term a national malaise. The future of the penny was up in the air, too.

Bicentennial Birthday Bash

Hmmm. How to celebrate your two-hundredth birthday? Fireworks would be nice. Red, white, and blue bunting sounds good—not to mention flag t-shirts, star-spangled tablecloths, and endless patriotic products. Oh, and what about a set of commemorative circulating coins?

It seems like all things American were on a downward trend in the 1970s, coin collecting among them. Numismatists urged the Mint to revive interest in coins by producing a revamped coin set for the Bicentennial year of 1976.

Sounds like a great idea, right? Not to the Mint. The Mint did not want to create another coin-hoarding frenzy like in the 1960s. In the great American tradition, a compromise was struck: The Mint would issue commemorative Bicentennial circulating dollar, half-dollar, and quarter coins. The dime, nickel, and penny would be left alone.

The Bicentennial Coinage Act of 1973 called for a design competition with a $5,000 prize. The winning designers also got to make trial strikes of their coins. The trial strikes were later destroyed. Or were they?

The Bicentennial coins were produced in large quantities so that they regularly circulated. Nearly 2 billion quarters were struck along with 500 million half-dollars and 250 million dollar coins. Millions of Americans became coin collectors—if only for the Bicentennial year. Plus, the seed was sown for the Mint's most ambitious coining program yet—the 50 State Quarters Program.

Now, about those trial strikes. Rumors abound that they're out there somewhere.

Bicentennial: The Mint's first foray into a circulating commemorative coinage celebrated the nation's Bicentennial. Quarters, half-dollars, and dollar coins were given new reverse artwork and were dated 1776-1976 to reflect 200 years of nationhood. (Photo Credit: R. Michael Field)

Denver kept its Mint and had it upgraded in 1983. Golf continues on the Park Hill Golf Course, which attracts players from all over the city. Freight trains still rumble past the dream site by the South Platte River, where the jingle of coins being spent can be heard from Six Flags Elitch Gardens, Coors Field, and a huge aquarium nearby. The Federal Center, dubbed Washington West, remains a major repository of federal records. And the Gates Rubber plant now houses an engineering and operations center for Qwest Communications, the local phone company.

We kept the penny, too.[6,7]

Chapter Notes

1. If you'd like to see Frank Gasparro's proposed design for a dollar coin with a flowing-haired Miss Liberty, check out home.earthlink.net/~smalldollars/dollar/page04.html.

2. A fun way to research the Susan B. Anthony dollar was to use it. Here's the report: Despite its unpopularity, it is still used by Denver's Light Rail system and was taken in highway tollbooths without a second glance. Clerks at convenience stores looked confused and wondered why we were giving them a quarter for two Hershey's bars.

3. There has been much written about the Susan B. Anthony dollar. Excellent overviews include the following articles: "The Susan B. Anthony Dollar 25 Years Later" by William E. Pike in *Numismatist* magazine, February 2004, pp. 31-33 and "The SBA Dollar: A Retrospective" by Jillian Leifer in *The Numismatist*, October 1998. Another good retrospective comes from the Web site www.maddys-treasure.com, and, of course, there's a lot of information on the Mint's official Web site, usmint.gov.

4. Rita Young at the Clayton Foundation (owners of the Park Hill Golf Course) gave us the lay of the land at the golf course and surrounding neighborhood.

5. Charlie Blosten, public service director of the City of Littleton, Colorado, filled in many details about the proposed conversion of the Gates facility in Littleton. He also shared helpful recollections of what Littleton was like in the 1970s.

6. The *Denver Post* and *Rocky Mountain News* covered the brouhaha over plans to relocate the Denver Mint from the late 1960s through the end of the debate more than a decade later in 1978. All the articles are available on

microfiche at the Denver Public Library. Or you can ask the wonderful librarians in the Western History Department. The file is called "Denver Federal Administration, Mint Building, 1970–1979."

7. The National Archives and Records Administration (NARA) has boxes of materials on the planned move. RG 104 is the reference number for Denver Mint materials. Ironically, the NARA is located at the Federal Center in Lakewood, Colorado, a site recommended for construction of the new Mint.

CHAPTER SEVEN

New, New, New for the Nineties (1990–2000)

American businesses—from major manufacturers to the corner hardware store—spent the nineties searching for secrets from gurus who had revitalized America's lackluster 1970s economy. The buzzwords for business and the US government by the nineties were bigger, faster, better, leaner, and meaner. You were only as good as your last product. And the Mint's last product was the Susan B. Anthony dollar.

The US Mint tackled the new decade with a passion for reinvention. This was not so easy for a centuries-old government institution. Like countless American businesses, the Mint examined its very identity. Was it simply a manufacturer taking orders from the Federal Reserve? Or was it a marketing-driven organization launching new products while cultivating new customers?

The Mint found it had one very large customer—the Federal Reserve—and millions of smaller customers—coin collectors and those of us who actually spent the coins. Collectors were particularly important, now that the coin shortage was long over, because when they added coins to their collections, they "bought" those coins and took them out of circulation. The Mint produced more coins to meet the demand, "selling" them to the Federal Reserve.

One problem: Collectors were growing older (the average coin collector was a man in his fifties), and new collectors weren't being minted, so to speak. Many collectors had lost interest when clad coins were introduced. Something had to change. The most obvious? The nation's coins.

Our coins had become boring. Phil Gramm, past chairman of the Senate Banking Committee, put it best when he said, "I think our coins and our currency are crummy."[1]

Coin presses calibrated to spot the tiniest discrepancies catch many errors. However, the eye of an experienced pressman may be the most important quality control in place at the Denver Mint. The press operator watches the coins as they roll into the catch basin. Because they see millions of coins in the course of each year, the smallest errors "jump out" at them, as one retired pressman told us at the Mint's Centennial Celebration. Flawed coins are plucked from the bin and sent to the "waffler," a massive press that defaces the coin by striking a deep waffle pattern onto each side. The Mint sends the waffled coins to its metal suppliers for recycling.

Once satisfied that the coins have passed inspection, the press operator discharges them into the counting and bagging area. (Photo Credit: US Mint)

So what? Aren't crummy coins accepted as readily as stunning silver ones designed by world-class engravers? Well, yes—but that's only part of the story. Coins do much more than merely facilitate commerce. Coins tell our common story, about who we are as a nation. An educational opportunity lies in every piece.

Coins also create relationships among citizens who share the milestones of history. Perhaps most poignantly, coins create bonds between generations, as a grandfather telling the story of what life was like when a Mercury dime or Kennedy half-dollar was struck.

Still not convinced of the power of coins? Consider this story, told by H. Robert Campbell, past president of the American Numismatic Association, at the Coin Design Symposium in 2000:

> My mother, Zoe Margerette Zetterborg, was born to a Russian father and Swedish mother. My mother's first impression of this great nation came from our coins. Holding a Walking Liberty half-dollar in her hand, she saw Miss Liberty draped in the American flag, her left hand clutching an olive branch close to her heart, demonstrating the importance of peace to the human soul. Liberty's right hand reaches out to a brilliant, new horizon, welcoming all who want to share the dream of this nation.
>
> The powerful symbols emblazoned on this silver coin offered the dream of liberty and the promise of freedom during the darkest days of World War II. It ignited a vision that one day she, like so many others before and after, would come to the United States of America. My mother desired a better place to raise her family; a place where freedom was not just an idea, and liberty and justice for all were more than just a dream.

Cursed Quarters? You Decide

Shortly after the 50 State Quarters program was instituted, misfortunes occurred connected to the images on the state quarters. Were these strange events a coincidence? Or is there, as some believe, a curse on the state quarters?

To protect yourself against the evil eye on these coins, find out how much you know about the curse of the quarters by taking the quiz below.

1. The unusual rock formation, known as the Old Man of the Mountain, was engraved onto the face of the New Hampshire quarter. Shortly afterwards, the face on the actual mountain:
   a. was found to be radioactive
   b. crumbled to the ground
   c. was destroyed in an earthquake (An earthquake in New Hampshire? Okay, this is an easy one.)

2. The Maryland quarter shows the statehouse in Annapolis— the oldest legislative building used as a capitol in the United States. In the summer of 2005:
   a. lightning struck and burned the building down
   b. lightning struck and ignited a fire that was put out safely
   c. lightning struck and scorched every politician inside the building (Wait—that wouldn't be a curse, would it?)

3. New Jersey's quarter pays homage to Washington's crossing of the Delaware. However, after the quarter came out, a reenactment of that crossing had to be cancelled because:
   a. the ACLU (American Civil Liberties Union) sued those reenacting the crossing because not enough women were involved in the event
   b. the man playing Washington fell into the water
   c. a terrible storm made the event unsafe

4. Rhode Island's quarter celebrates sailing. However, in 2005 the famous America's Cup was not won by an American team, but by:
   a. Switzerland, a totally land-locked country
   b. Chile, a country with 2,650 miles of coastline
   c. Vatican City, the smallest country in the world

(continued on next page)

5. Helen Keller graces Alabama's coin. A revival of the play "The Miracle Worker," which tells the story of Keller:
   a. bombed on Broadway the same day the coin was struck
   b. was turned into a perky musical, which many viewers found offensive
   c. closed before it even made it to Broadway

6. Two quarters—North Carolina and Ohio—claim the fame of the Wright Brothers. Only one problem:
   a. speculation that the Wright brothers didn't make the first flight but were beaten to it by a New Zealand farmer
   b. nobody wants to celebrate that the first flight was ever taken because of the long lines and bad food associated with modern flights
   c. diaries of the Wright Brothers were recently found where they said they despised both North Carolina and Ohio

7. The Carolina Wren, a quintessential Southern bird that perches on South Carolina's quarter, has:
   a. become extinct
   b. lost its feathers because of an increase in the already muggy humidity of South Carolina
   c. recently been spotted nesting in locations as far north as Rhode Island and Ontario, Canada

Answer Key:
1—b; 2—b; 3—c; 4—a; 5—c; 6—a; 7—c
How many did you get correct? See the legend below to determine your aptitude for curses:

6–7 correct: Congratulations! You are an expert.

4–5 correct: Okay, but you could use a little work. Get some state quarters and study them thoroughly.

2–3 correct: Sign up for Curses 101 at your local community college.

0–1 correct: Just spend the quarters and forget about curses altogether.

Disclaimer: All of the above scourges, hexes, and tribulations actually happened. There's some speculation that the curse comes from George Washington himself—or at least his ghost who's angry because the size of his portrait on the coins has been made smaller. Just dumb luck? Or is the curse real? [2]

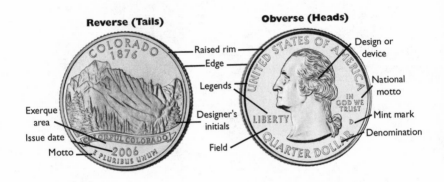

Reverse (Tails)   **Obverse (Heads)**

COLORADO 1876

Raised rim
Edge
Legends
Designer's initials
Field

Exerque area
Issue date
Motto

COLORFUL COLORADO
2006
E PLURIBUS UNUM

UNITED STATES OF AMERICA
IN GOD WE TRUST
LIBERTY
D
QUARTER DOLLAR

Design or device
National motto
Mint mark
Denomination

Know Heads From Tails: There are two sides to every coin, right? Wrong! Try three sides, including the edge. (Photo Credit: U.S. Mint)

She had to trade that half dollar, a few other silver coins and pieces of dinnerware for a 20-pound bag of potatoes and a few eggs to help sustain her family during the war. However, she never lost hope because that sliver of silver provided a tangible link to the place my mother eventually would call home.[3]

Campbell went on to say that he didn't consider most of our coins worthy of our nation. During the nineties, many agreed with Campbell. Collectors, politicians, and everyday citizens found our coinage uninspired. Common complaints included the metallic composition of clad coins, the cluttered appearance of the face of coins, and their boring designs.

It's no surprise that we found ourselves yawning over our coins. All of them, except the dollar, have hung around longer than twenty-five years—for some, twice as long. The Lincoln cent has remained the same since 1909—longer than any other coin in US history. The Washington quarter hasn't changed since 1932, the Jefferson nickel since 1938, the dime since 1946, and the Kennedy half-dollar since 1964.

Customers bored with the product? A shrinking customer base of collectors? Clearly, dramatic action was called for. The Mint set out on a mission to reawaken America's passion for coins.

The Mint on a Mission

The US Mint's product is one that people can touch and hold. And it produces a profit.

But this is the US government. It can't simply call profit by the term the rest of the business world uses. In the world of minting, it's called *seigniorage*. Seigniorage is the difference between the face value of the coin and the cost to produce it. For example, it costs the Mint less than five cents to make a quarter, so the seigniorage for that coin is around twenty cents.

The Federal Reserve pays the coins' face value when it buys them for distribution to banks. Subtract the cost to make the coins—materials, labor, manufacturing, transportation, and general administrative costs of running the Mint—and you have the seigniorage amount, or the Mint's profit. Seigniorage ranges from a few tenths of a cent on the penny to around 80 cents on dollar coins. This profit is returned to the US Treasury general fund.

When you think of the profit the Mint generates by introducing new coin designs, the wisdom of reigniting a passion for coins makes a lot of sense. As American manufacturers know, whether they're talking laundry soap

The Quintessential Denver Omelet

At Dozens Restaurant the traditional Denver omelet is called "Imagine a Great Omelet." *5280* magazine named Dozens's Denver omelet the best in town. They've been serving it one city block from the Denver Mint for almost twenty years. The Denver omelet is traditionally a three- or four-egg omelet (depending on the size of the eggs) with ham, onion, green pepper, mushroom, and cheese as the usual fillings. Amounts shown below are approximate—make according to your own taste. Here's how Dozens prepares its famous omelet.

Ingredients:
4 large eggs
¼ cup onion
¼ to ½ cup green bell peppers
¼ to ½ cup mushrooms
½ cup cooked ham, diced
Margarine, melted
4 ounces Swiss cheese
½ teaspoon salt
½ teaspoon pepper

(continued on next page)

or computers, the best way to spur sales is to introduce a new product.[4]

A Golden Plan

When casting their eyes for a new product, the US Mint decided upon a dollar coin. The Mint approached the new dollar like any other consumer products company. Market research came first. The Mint conducted focus groups and surveyed Americans to find out what they wanted in a new coin.

The Treasury Department then appointed a nine-member committee to recommend a design for the obverse (heads) of the new coin. (The US One Dollar Coin Act of 1997, the law

Prep:

1. Beat your eggs and add about 1 teaspoon of water per serving.

2. Julienne chop green pepper and quality precooked ham. Slice mushrooms and onions. Lightly sauté the vegetables and keep warm. Grate Swiss cheese.

3. Add ham to your sautéed veggies and turn the heat up to medium. Using an 8- or 9-inch nonstick pan, turn on high heat and add margarine. When the margarine is bubbling, pour in the eggs. Let the eggs cook until a firm edge has developed around the entire omelet. Use a rubber spatula to pull the edge toward the middle while tipping the pan, allowing the raw egg to fill the space. Repeat three or four times from side to side. Let cook for about 10 more seconds. Turn off burner then repeat the spatula trick until almost all the raw egg is cooked. Quickly add the cheese first, and then the rest of the fillings along a line down the middle of the omelet. Tilt the pan over the plate until the edge of the omelet touches the plate. Now roll the omelet over itself. If the egg is soft and not browned with deep crevices caused by the spatula trick, you did great. Dozens serves theirs with a buttered English muffin, breakfast potatoes, and a slice of fresh fruit.

Golden Dollar Obverse © 1999 United States Mint. Used with permission.

authorizing the design and development of the Golden Dollar, specified that the coin carry the depiction of an eagle on the reverse.) The committee decided that a woman should be depicted on the coin. Some of the females who were considered include the following: Clara Barton, Shirley Chisholm, Emma Lazarus (poet), Juliette Gordon Low (founder of the Girl Scouts), Rosa Parks, Betsy Ross, Nellie Ross (the first woman governor), Eleanor Roosevelt, Margaret Chase Smith (the first woman to be elected to both houses of Congress), Sacajawea, Harriet Tubman, Sojourner Truth, Martha Washington, and Mary Ball Washington (George Washington's mother). Eventually, they recommended Sacajawea.[5]

The choice drew mixed reviews. Promoters of the coin cheered its political correctness and the depiction of a Native American. The most outspoken was First Lady Hillary Clinton, who said in April 1999 at the White House ceremony announcing the new coin, "How fitting that the first US coin of the new millennium should carry the image of the Native American woman whose courage and quiet dignity provides such a powerful link to our past. The Sacajawea coin honors an extraordinary woman who helped shape the history of our nation and preserves her important legacy for future generations."

Its detractors were less excited. Native Americans had often been featured on American coins, they said, so what was the big deal? The choice was too politically correct and screamed of tokenism.

Representative Michael N. Castle of Delaware tried to have the choice replaced with the Statue of Liberty, citing the fact that she would be more easily recognized. Indian groups countered that Sacajawea would be recognized far more readily if her image were on the dollar.

In an even harsher response, a June 1998 article in the

Minneapolis Star said, "The new coin was supposed to bear the image of an American woman who took a stand for liberty and justice. And the only woman they could name was a poor girl recorded in history for her ability to beat dirty laundry on a rock?"[6]

Despite objections, Sacajawea remained the woman of choice for the Golden Dollar (so named because of its golden sheen). The Mint invited twenty-three artists to submit designs. They were not given extensive guidelines but were told to concentrate on cultural sensitivity and historical accuracy (a tall order since no likeness of Sacajawea exists).

The Mint went to new heights of consumer involvement by posting the design finalists on the Internet and soliciting public response. The result: 120,000 e-mails and 2,000 letters. The Mint was astonished by the response.

The Mint also showed the designs to Native American tribal leaders and members of Congress. They conducted focus groups with public citizens and coin experts and solicited input from historians.

Glenna Goodacre won the final prize for the depiction of Sacajawea. The coin was unveiled at a lofty ceremony on May 4, 1999, complete with representatives from several Native American tribes, Native drumming, Goodacre and her Shoshone model, and political dignitaries.

The Mint successfully sold the coin to Powers-that-Be and 140,000 interested citizens. But a bigger undertaking lay ahead: to sell the coin to John Q. Public.

Taking a page from consumer marketing companies, the Mint embarked upon an innovative promotional campaign for the Golden Dollar. A 2000 Golden Dollar was packed into every two-thousandth "specially marked box" of Cheerios breakfast cereal. Full-page ads featuring George Washington appeared in mainstream magazines such as *People*. The popular TV game show *Wheel of Fortune* awarded a cache of

Glenna Goodacre at work on the Sacagawea Dollar designs with her model Randy L'Teton. (Photo Credit: Doug Merriam)

Glenna Goodacre in her Santa Fe studio at work on the Sacagawea obverse in the 8-inch coin basin from the Mint. All U.S. coins start with a coin basin like this. (Photo Credit: Daniel Anthony)

the coins as a prize—under the watchful eye of the Mint police.

Public relations or "free" marketing opportunities were added to the mix. Appearances by Glenna Goodacre, members of the Native American community, and the President and Mrs. Clinton generated stories in print and broadcast media. Even the delivery of the sculptor's fee was turned into a media opportunity, as the Mint police showed up at Glenna Goodacre's Santa Fe studio with five thousand Golden Dollars. The cameras, of course, were rolling.

The launch of the Golden Dollar was a success by any standard. But the hoopla faded in comparison to the largest and most ambitious product innovation in Mint history—the 50 State Quarter Program.

Turning a Quarter Into Billions of Dollars

In 1996 Congress passed the US Commemorative Coin Act, calling for each state to be commemorated with its own unique quarter. Fifty new coin designs would be struck over a ten-year period, with five designs being produced each year. The coins would debut in the order the state entered the union. At the end of each coin's ten-week run, it would not be produced again. Furthermore, the states would participate in the design of the new coins. Congress left it to the Mint to make it happen, and they started printing the quarters in 1999.

The Mint started by talking to its customers—ordinary Americans—through surveys and focus groups. Was there interest in such a program? What design themes would be popular? And the all-important question: Would Americans collect the new coins?

The answer was a resounding *yes*.[7]

The Mint put a huge marketing push behind the 50 State Quarters Program. The directive was clear: Make quarters cool to kids and their parents. Kermit the Frog was called in as celebrity spokesperson—er, spokesfrog—in print advertising and television. The Mint partnered with retail giants such as Wal-Mart to distribute the coins with a promotional salvo that would rival anything Madison Avenue could produce.

The US Postal Service paired with the Mint and packaged state stamps with state quarters. In heartland fashion, the two entities announced the program at the Mall of America in Minneapolis. Miss America 2003 was even in attendance. Not only did the partnership introduce a unique collectible, it provided the opportunity to use the words "numismatist" and "philatelist" in the same sentence!

The program has exceeded all expectations. Sounding more like a giddy dot-commer than the head of a government agency, former Mint Director Philip N. Diehl described the program in 1999: "How many companies have introduced a product that will sell more than four billion units in its first year and will be touched by every person in the country? When you think of it in those terms, this program is huge. Even if you think of it in profit terms, it's huge."[8]

Halfway through its run, the 50 State Quarters Program has generated more than $4.6 billion in seigniorage. It is estimated that 130 million Americans, or one per household, collect state quarters.[9] Best of all, Americans are looking at their change more closely.

Telling Every State's Story. States selected images and designs to encapsulate the state's unique story. (Photo Credit: U.S. Mint)

Glenna Goodacre

Each day sculptor Glenna Goodacre walks next door to her studio from her adobe home in the pinon-scented hills above Santa Fe, New Mexico. Her two poodles, Chaco and Camille, saunter along beside her as she passes buckets of flowers and the bronze sculptures of smiling children for which she is known. Along the way she might spy a yellow flower showing off on a cholla cactus or a tawny lizard basking in the New Mexican sunshine. Cozy antique furniture fills her studio, and a fire crackles in a corner fireplace during winter months. Bookshelves are loaded with art books and, of course, sculptures. Large, serrated kitchen knives—her favorite sculpting tools—sit atop counters. Once inside, Glenna begins her day's work: sculpting a life-sized figure or molding a small bronze.

Glenna is one of a few gifted sculptures who have the luxury of choosing what she will work on. She has achieved a prestige in the art world that most artists only aspire to. She has more than fifty bronze portraits in public collections throughout the United States and has won many awards.

Yet it is possible for everyone to own one of her works. We can all get our hands on the Sacajawea Golden Dollar. Glenna designed the image of Sacajawea and her infant son, Jean Baptiste, for the US Mint. We talked to her on a sunny autumn day and she told us, hints of a Texas drawl in her voice, about her experience in the coin business.

Q: How did you find out about the new dollar coin?

A: I read three sentences in *USA Today*. A committee had selected Sacajawea to replace the Susan B. Anthony dollar. I submitted six designs; 121 designs were submitted to the Mint by a total of twenty-three artists. Mint officials collected public response on a Web site, then narrowed it down to six finalists.

Q: We understand the six semifinalists were all yours.

A: Yes.

Q: Was it Sacajawea that sparked your interest?

A: Yes. I'd read a big, thick novel on Sacajawea so I knew a lot about her. And the beauty of my experience was, because I am a bona fide sculptor, they asked me if I'd like to do my own work.

(continued on next page)

Usually they design a coin and the engravers in Philadelphia do the work. I dropped everything I was doing to do that artwork.

Q: So it seems like your role went from designer to actually sculpting it.

A: Yes, and I got to sign it.

Q: Did you decide to put the baby on it or was that the Mint's choice?

A: In my research I was most impressed with Sacajawea's youth and the fact that she carried a baby all the way to the Pacific and back. I thought that was an important part of her story.

Q: Yes, little Jean Baptiste turned into an important ambassador himself.

A: The secretary of the Treasury had the final say, and he asked if I could do it without the baby. So I scraped off the baby and sent pictures to Washington. But everyone liked the baby. So I put him back on. That's a first in coinage. But that was part of the whole story. To do a three-quarter image of her looking back was entirely different. It was criticized by other designers, who said it wouldn't wear well. But an artist gets criticized on all fields anyway.

Q: The Susan B. Anthony dollar was criticized because of the appearance of Susan B. Anthony. Was there any pressure to make a "pretty" image of Sacajawea?

A: That was my choice. My model was pretty. Nobody knows what Sacajawea looked like. My model was Shoshone, which was the tribe Sacajawea was from.

Q: The Mint did a lot of market research on what Americans wanted in a dollar coin. As an artist, did they give you that market research, and was it restricting to work to those specs?

A: The engraving department at the Mint sets the specs and restrictions. I was given a concave block of plaster. I brought it back here to Santa Fe and we worked on an 8-inch round. The thickest part was only an eighth of an inch thick, so when I did the first coin and they struck it, she looked like she was about eighty-five years old. So I did it over and over—I think about seven times. But always within their strict specifications. It was an educational process that I thoroughly enjoyed. But I have yet to

(continued on next page)

make another one.

Q: Were you expecting the reaction people had to Sacajawea?

A: I was flattered because the majority of the coins are going into safes and bottom drawers. People collect them. That's a very big compliment to me, though they have quit minting them. They're not profitable for the Mint, and the Mint is a profit organization. That is disappointing. But as a collector's item they are going up in value.

Q: As you were thinking about designing the coin, did you ever think about children, maybe budding coin collectors, looking at your work?

A: Yes, and I think that will be a lasting tribute to Lewis and Clark. Sacajawea was chosen because she was a hero among women. The stories are great about what she did and will remain forever. So if nothing else, it's an educational coin about part of our American history.

Q: Native Americans have strong, positive feelings about this coin, right?

A: Oh, yes. They're very flattered to be on it.

Q: What kinds of things did they say to you personally?

A: Oh, all compliments. We had a big ceremony at the White House and different tribes were there with drums. It was good for everybody, especially me because I get to go in the Redbook forever, and that's the Bible for coin collectors.

Q: We read that you said you've never received a Sacajawea in change.

A: I have never received one. Do you know how many people have never heard of the coin? I was at a big hotel and gave the coin as a tip to a maid. I said, "I sculpted this." She looked at me and said, "Uh huh." I'm sure she didn't think it was real.

Q: Maybe she thought it was a little sample of your work.

A: She didn't even think that. She just thought she'd been hoodwinked. That's the way it goes. When traveling I always carry a roll with me and I give them as tips. People have never seen them.

Q: Too bad. It's probably their only opportunity to own a Glenna Goodacre.

A (laughs): They don't know me.

(continued on next page)

Q: We saw that you were paid your commission in Sacajawea coins.

A: Yes, and that got blown so out of proportion. It was just a passing thought. Why should I receive a check? They owed me $5,000 for my design. I wanted to wait 'til the coins came out and take it in coins. Is that sinister?

Q: No!

A: Then it all hit the fan when I decided to sell. These were all first-strike coins. The Mint used their delivery as a publicity thing. They came to the studio with a couple of guards and they dumped the coins on the table at my studio. So then I got the idea—actually, it was not my idea—a coin collector gave me the idea to sell them, because they're a collector's item. But the press decided that was tacky. You may have read those articles.

Q: We didn't think it was tacky at all. We thought it was smart. Do you have any more plans to revisit Sacajawea in the future?

A: No, I think I've worn her out.

Q. We're wondering what you're working on now?

A. I'm doing some smaller pieces that I've wanted to do. I'm not accepting many commissions. I'm just doing what I want. [10]

Chapter Notes

1. Speeches given at the Senate Banking Committee Coin Design Symposium are available online at http://banking.senate.gov/coin2000/coin-sym.htm.

2. The shocking claims about the curse of the state quarters can be found in an entertaining article, "The Curse of the Quarter," by Gordon T. Anderson on CNNMoney.com. We bring it to you as a public service.

3. H. Robert Campbell, past president of the American Numismatic Association, graciously granted permission to share the story of his mother.

4. The *Annual Report* is the best, most reliable source for production figures, costs, seigniorage, management, custodial gold and silver reserves, and general questions about the day-to-day business of running the US Mint. We used the annual reports dating back to 1906 for information about construction, renovation, and workforce issues throughout the century.

5. The US Mint's Web site (www.usmint.gov) provides an excellent chronology of how the Golden Dollar came into being.

6. Information about the negative reaction to the Sacajawea coin was found on the following Web site: http://womenshistory.about.com/od/sacagawea/a/sacagawea_3.htm.

7. Consumer research and projections regarding the 50 State Quarters Program are found in the program's feasibility study, *50 States Commemorative Coin Program Study*, by Coopers & Lybrand, May 30, 1997.

8. Mint Director Philip N. Diehl's giddy quote about the "huge" success of the 50 State Quarters Program

appeared in the article "Mint Condition" by Anna Muoio in the business magazine *Fast Company* in December 1999.

9. The goal and productivity numbers in this chapter were taken from *The US Mint Strategic Plan 2002–2007* and the *US Mint 2004 Annual Report*. The astounding assertion that "more than 130 million Americans collect 50 State Quarters" appears here.

10. In November 2005 we interviewed Glenna Goodacre about her role in designing the Golden Dollar. She was chatty and personable, and we appreciate her spending time with us. Her assistant, Daniel R. Anthony, has also been very helpful by providing information, sending photos, and answering questions.

CHAPTER EIGHT

The New Millennium at the Mint (2000 and Beyond)

It might be an historic edifice patterned after a Florentine palace, but the Mint is still a modern factory like any other. Well, maybe not like any other.

Behind the Scenes at the Mint

Visitors to the Mint watch the action from a soundproof, glassed-in balcony. It's quiet and climate-controlled, and the tour guide is an expert who can tell you everything you'd ever want to know. But what's it like to be surrounded by money all day? (And all night, since the Mint runs night shifts as well.)

Come along and find out.

The first thing you notice when you go onto the manufacturing floor is that it's scrupulously clean. There are no smells of chemicals or dust. No mucky buckets of oily black liquid. No messy piles of scrap metal cluttering the floor.

The only clutter is money. Coins are occasionally scattered on the floor beside the buckets that catch them as they are spit from the machines. But in a place like this, what are a few stray coins?

Money is everywhere. Enormous barrels are full of it, and a solid stream of coins flies from the machines every second. Vast vats are filled with shiny pennies, some that have already been printed with Lincoln's image, some that are blanks. Big pails hold the latest state quarter. There are even tubs of rippled coins that have been "waffled"—coins condemned to the waffler because of errors. The money is warm to the touch, although the factory floor is a little chilly when a winter breeze wafts through.

Three Generations of Mint Construction: Though separated by nearly a century, the additions of the late 1990s and the 2001 entrance, complement each other. (Photo Credit: R. Michael Field)

Even though you're wearing earplugs, you'll hear the noise. It's the sound of industry. Machines growl as they cleave through sheets of metal. Coins clink as they land in the bins. Workers carry on conversations, and occasionally you'll hear the hoot of a forklift as it crosses the floor, loaded with a keg of coins.

The colors inside the Mint may surprise you. You might expect dull shades of gray and brown. But the vats holding the pennies are vivid orange, as if color-coded with the burnished russet of the coins. Bright yellow signs and pathways painted on the floor direct forklift drivers. Cobalt-blue barrels that store chemicals and cleaners sit on the sidelines, and even the coin-making machines are trimmed in royal-blue sound buffers. Rose-colored containers are attached to the walls to hold safety glasses and earplugs.

At the Mint, machinery and metal overshadow everything else. Huge black coils hang from the ceiling like giant snakes. Enormous rolls of metal are stored in the corners as they wait to be punched into coins. Monster machines chop through metal like giant mechanical cookie cutters.

Then you come to the bagging room and machines are not so predominant. The machines are still there, but what you notice are piles of white bags with big blue straps. These are the "money bags." They're probably far bigger than you'd imagine, about the size of a card table. They hold between 200,000 and 500,000 coins. When full, they weigh between 2,200 and 2,600 pounds, depending on which coins are inside. Not exactly something you could tuck under your arm and walk away with! [1]

Of course, the machines aren't the most important workers in the Mint, despite their imposing size. *People* run those machines—Mint workers, who have a few special rules. Each work day, for instance, Mint employees pass through metal detectors and x-ray machines, similar to those you'd

Up to 500,000 coins are dropped into one money bag, which weighs over a ton. The money bags are weighed, sealed shut and loaded onto pallets. They are shipped to a Federal Reserve branch in non-descript semi-trucks where they are stored in vaults until needed.

Just think, the next plain-looking tractor-trailer rig you see on the highway might be loaded with millions of coins from the Denver Mint! (Photo Credit: US Mint)

find in an airport. They do this after they empty their pockets of coins. No coins go in, and no coins go out. Workers toss their change onto the table at Dozens, a nearby restaurant, because they can carry only bills back to work. The windfall in tips to the servers at the restaurant is a long-running joke.

On the factory floor, employees work amid coin presses that clatter like drunken slot machines. Strip away the glamour of all that money, and you have a factory dealing with the same issues you'd find in any plant. The Mint moves to the rhythm of productivity goals, error reports, and inventory turns. Safety is of paramount importance. Occupational Safety and Health Administration (OSHA) requirements are strictly enforced, and accident statistics are carefully tracked.

The Mint is home to a diverse, unionized workforce represented by the American Federation of Government Workers, Local 695. The age-old dance of labor and management goes on, including accusations of sexual harassment that have resulted in four lawsuits and more than a hundred formal complaints. A class action suit filed in July 2003 alleged sexual harassment, gender discrimination, and retaliation at the Denver Mint. In March 2006 the US Mint, while denying liability, settled the class action suit with a $9 million payout, shared by the 132 claimants.[2]

Providing a quality workplace is a serious goal for the Mint and is included in its mission statement. The Denver Mint hosts sensitivity training and wellness clinics offering employees stress reduction techniques, massage therapy, and healthy eating workshops.

Working at the Mint is considered one of the best manufacturing jobs in Denver. Many employees spend their entire careers there, although Mint workers sometimes worry that "politics" will cause the Mint to close or relocate.

Corn Mint Salad

1 16-ounce bag frozen sweet white corn
1 diced red pepper
1 diced orange pepper
1 cup canned black beans (rinsed)
Juice of 1 lime
1 bunch fresh mint, coarsely chopped

Combine all ingredients and toss.
Keeps really well on a buffet table.
Great potluck dish!

Security for employees at the Denver Mint is tighter than in most businesses. One contractor who works with the Mint claims that security requirements are tighter than even the US military. Anyone doing business with the Mint must be willing to undergo a background check. The vigilance can be wearing on employees, so the Mint is working to develop security measures that will be more transparent to its workers. [3]

The money surrounding Mint employees becomes abstract after a while. Indeed, most have no idea just how much gold is there. But the pride the Denver Mint employees have in their centuries-old task is very real.

New Coins for a New Millennium

Coins may once again be "cool" as we head into the Denver Mint's second century. Perhaps the new interest in coins (and the Mint's phenomenal profitability) will spark another Golden Age of Coin Design, as numismatists refer to the early twentieth century. Teddy Roosevelt, US president at the time and an avid coin collector, helped establish this era. He asked renowned US sculptor Augustus Saint-Gaudens to design new coins that would appropriately reflect American greatness. The president corresponded with the sculptor over several months, exchanging ideas and sharing complaints about resistance to the radical new designs.

The Most Beautiful Coin? Augustus Saint-Gaudens' $20 gold coin depicting Liberty with flowing hair, striding forward is considered the most attractive coin ever minted in the United States. Saint-Gaudens died August 3, 1907 and never saw any of his double eagles circulated. Charles E. Barber prepared a low relief model from Saint-Gaudens' designs. The design was poorly suited to mass production and discontinued. (Photo Credit: greattoning, from Coin Page)

New Threats in a New Millennium

Picture this: George Clooney and Brad Pitt, lounging on the patio of some trendy Denver eatery, gazing through their wraparound sunglasses at the sunset over the snowy peaks of the Rocky Mountains. In a witty exchange, they plot their next caper for *Ocean's 23*, a heist of the gold repository at the Denver Mint.

Enter William F. Daddio, associate director for protection/ chief of US Mint police. When asked about this very scenario, he laughed and said, "They'd lose."

George, Brad, and the boys aren't very high on Bill Daddio's threat matrix. He spends his days thinking about far more sobering concerns.

In kinder, gentler times, the main worry at the Denver Mint was theft. "We used to stay within the gates," Daddio said. "We drew up the drawbridge, heated the oil, and got the alligators ready for the night." But since the Oklahoma City bombing in 1994, the Denver Mint, like all federal buildings, now looks beyond its perimeter to detect potential attacks—real and symbolic—to both the Mint facility and its employees.

The Mint is located in an urban center, across the street from the County Courthouse. The new Denver police station and jail are slated for construction on the west side of the Mint. Daddio is pleased with his neighbors because he likes having more law enforcement eyes on the Mint. But one can't help but think that he would sleep better if the Mint were located out on the wide prairie, with nothing but tumbleweeds coming within miles.

The Mint maintains its own security force of highly qualified individuals, the Mint police. It is an elite force. Basic requirements include a college degree in a criminal justice field (or three years of law enforcement experience), extensive

(continued on next page)

training, and a yearlong apprenticeship. Mint police must qualify for a sharpshooter ranking every six months, which means target practice in the basement gunnery range is a part of everyday life for members of the force.

Far from simply guarding the gold, US Mint Special Response Teams regularly undertake other duties, such as acting as a security force at the presidential inauguration in 2001. In the fall of 2005, Mint police were dispatched to New Orleans to secure the money supply in the wake of Hurricane Katrina.

But they never forget about the gold. The federal government doesn't transport gold much any more, but when it does, the Mint police rely on heavy and overt security.

The Mint police also focus on cyber security. Computer security systems are isolated, so there's no threat of crooks hacking into the vault codes. Mint police guard against computer crimes, with programs designed to catch such activity by monitoring any differences or changes made to Mint records. Today, for instance, an employee could never change inventory numbers, then try to sneak a few bars out of the Mint, as Orville did so many years ago.

Perhaps the most important job for the Mint police is anticipating threats to our nation's security. A simple gold heist, à la *Ocean's 11* or *Goldfinger,* seems tame in a world of terrorism. Now identifying the adversary is a complex, ever-changing game with very real consequences. The Mint must defend against explosive, chemical, as well as biological attacks—all while maintaining its status as a tourist attraction in an urban neighborhood.

One comes away from a conversation with Daddio confident that America's wealth is well protected. But one can't help but feel nostalgic for the days when the threat came from a quiet man with a wooden leg.

Denver's Victorian boosters got their wish of an imposing mint complete with lawn and trees that would become a focal point for the city. The Denver Mint's impressive façade fronts West Colfax Avenue. Stretching from mountain to plain, Colfax is called Denver's Main Street.

The Colfax façade no longer serves as the main entrance to the Mint. The employee and business entrance lies around the corner in a twenty-first century addition that accommodates the security and screening equipment though which all must pass on their way into and out of the Mint.

Visitors on organized tours exit the building through the heavy bronze doors. They pass chinks in the marble of the Grand Gallery where bullets from the robbery of 1923 tore through this doorway. (Photo Credit: David Hall)

Saint-Gaudens produced a coin that would become known as the most attractive piece ever minted in the United States: a twenty-dollar gold coin bearing the image of Liberty holding a torch and striding forward. In a letter to Roosevelt dated November 11, 1905, Saint-Gaudens called it "a living thing and typical of progress." It took several strikes to make the coins, however, so production was slow. President Roosevelt ordered the Mint to "begin the new issue even if it takes you one day to strike one piece!" Unfortunately, Roosevelt failed to find continued support for his passion in coins after Saint-Gaudens died in 1907. [4]

Roosevelt might not be happy with some of today's coins, but he would undoubtedly be pleased with current Mint trends. The Mint is creating new coins for the new millennium—new designs, new series, new commemoratives.

For starters, nickels have gotten an extreme makeover. The Westward Journey series released two new designs in 2004 and two more in 2005. A close profile of Jefferson's right side is shown, while the opposite side features a buffalo or the Pacific Ocean and the words "Ocean in view! O' The Joy!" The words come from the journal of William Clark, written when he reached the Columbia River after the arduous Lewis and Clark journey. The westward expansion series is a temporary issue, but a permanent redesign of the nickel is also planned.

Another new series is slated for that much-maligned and unsuccessful coin: the dollar. The new coins will feature presidents who have been dead for longer than two years. (Living people are not featured on US coins.) The reverse of the dollar will show the Statue of Liberty. Four coins a year will be issued, starting in 2007, in the presidents' order of service. It is reasonable to assume that the dollars will become another popular collector's item and thus will make a lot of money for the Mint.

Along with these coins, even the good old Lincoln penny is slated for a makeover. A brand new penny is in the works to commemorate the two-hundredth anniversary of Lincoln's birth and one hundred years of the Lincoln penny. Surely even Abe would agree it's time for a new look. In 2009 four

Chicanery in the Corn?

Every now and then an error finds its way out of the Denver Mint, much to the delight of coin collectors. Take, for example, the 2004-D Wisconsin state quarter.

In December 2004, sharp-eyed collectors in Tucson, Arizona, and San Antonio, Texas, spotted strange goings-on in their change. It seemed the ear of corn on the Wisconsin state quarter had sprouted an extra leaf or two. There are two types of extra leaf error: the high leaf, which points upward, and the low leaf drooping downward.

How did the extra foliage get there? Some experts believe the culprit was metal shavings lodged in the die. When the coins were struck, the shavings gouged the die, leaving a raised scratch on the coin. On close inspection, these extra "leaves" do not meet the design quality of the rest of the image.

The extra "leaves" leap out of enlarged photographs but are difficult to see with the naked eye on the quarters. It's not hard to imagine such a tiny defect escaping an inspector's scrutiny. And with billions of state quarters produced, some errors are bound to happen.

But does something more sinister lurk in the corn?

Many numismatists are certain that the "leaves" were a deliberate addition by someone at the Denver Mint. They argue that the odds of such convenient placement are simply too great to be random. An amateur engraver had to be behind it. Numismatists say it might have happened like this: A Mint employee doctors a die with an engraving tool, slips the die onto the press, and then removes it after the coins are struck. The die is destroyed with other worn-out dies.

(continued on next page)

pennies will be issued reflecting the four major periods in Lincoln's life. Coin collectors take note: Quantities of the new copper pennies will have the same metallic content as the 1909 penny.

The Mint is not only interested in the appearance, artistic

The question is why? The Mint's state-of-the-art security measures prevent employees from taking coins out of the Mint. Finished coins are shipped to the Federal Reserve for distribution. Mint workers have no knowledge where coins might wind up or even when coins will be placed into circulation. What would be the motivation for a Mint employee to risk a coveted job to create such an error?

Perhaps someone wanted to make their mark on coins. Or maybe someone took the personal challenge to beat security and smuggle a valuable error out of the Mint. Maybe someone was watching for his or her handiwork in every pocketful of change.

At the height of the corn frenzy, sets containing both errors were selling for more than $1,500. But just like with Beanie Babies, prices cooled off—although a set sold recently on eBay for $2,800.

Here's the official explanation from the Treasury Department's office of inspector general, as reported in *USA Today:* "A press operator at the Denver Mint working on a Friday night in November 2004 noticed blemishes on coins produced at one of the five presses he was operating. He stopped the machine and left for a meal break. He returned to find the machine running and assumed someone else changed the die. During a regular inspection, the operator realized the die had not been changed. The press likely had been operating for ninety minutes, and thousands of coins were commingled with unblemished quarters." The Mint opted not to hand-sort the blemished quarters or to destroy the entire bag, which was ready to be shipped, because it would be too costly. No one was fired because of the incident.

The Mint investigated and believes the leafy quarters are simply mistakes. What do you think? [5]

Return to Monticello: On the 2006 nickel, President Thomas Jefferson's image was inspired by an 1800 painting by Rembrandt Peale. (Photo Credit: Courtesy of the U.S. Mint)

value, and seigniorage of the new coins. The Mint works closely with educators to create teaching aids. We all are learning about America as we discover peace medals, long boats, and other historic relics of the Lewis and Clark Expedition on our nickels.

Our coins have become a visual representation of our nation's motto *E Pluribus Unum,* or "out of many, one." And the value of that can't be measured in terms of seigniorage.

2006: Centennial Celebration

They greet each other with handshakes and back slaps. Happy to see each other, they joke and reminisce. They admire the party decorations and pick up chocolate pennies from the balloon-dressed tables. But they do not bring presents to this birthday party, for *they* are the guests of honor.

It is the Denver Mint's centennial celebration, but the focus is not on the historic building or the billions upon billions of coins that were made there. It is a celebration of everyone who has worked in its pressrooms, melting rooms, weighing rooms, and offices over the past century.

Denver Mayor John Hickenlooper proclaimed February 1, 2006, the US Mint in Denver Day. On that day exactly one century earlier, the Mint struck its first coins using three coining presses.

"I am humbled by the thousands of years of service in this room," Plant Manager Tim Riley told the 550 current and former employees. "Today we pay tribute to our craft and to the artisans of the coins that jingle in the pockets and purses of nearly every American."

The employees and retirees shared stories of the more recent history of the Mint. Fletcher Johnson, who retired in 1975, spoke of being one of a handful of African-American

A Time Capsule to Be Opened in 2106 Awaits Future Mint Employees and History Buffs: Plant Manager Tim Riley places a scroll signed by current Mint employees into a time capsule as U. S. Mint Acting Director looks on. The time capsule, to be opened on February 1, 2106 contains the scroll with employee signatures and a message, City of Denver Mayoral Proclamation declaring February 1, 2006 "United States Mint at Denver Day," and a set of 2006 uncirculated coins minted in Denver. (Photo Credit: Kimberly Field)

employees when he started in 1961 as a punch press operator. He trained to become a machinist and served as president of the Union.

One pressman laughed that after thirty years in the Mint he no longer needed to use a magnifying glass to spot errors on coins. Even the tiniest errors jumped out at him.

John Chacon, who started in the deposit melting room in 1960, shared his career memories of working with the gold. He recalled placing gold bars in the vaults. He wrote his initials on the labels attached to the vault before they were marked with wax seals. During his thirty-year career, he melted gold and cast bars. "I felt proud as I held the gold bars. It was something I made."

Retirees marveled at the changes at the Mint. Chacon said, "I worked in the sweeps cellar, and it was a dirty old hole. Now it's a nice, clean lunchroom."

After the ceremony, retirees filed out through security, laughing and joking as the Mint police carefully screened everyone. One retiree took off his belt and placed it in a basket to pass through the x-ray machine, like one would do in a modern airport. The belt, festooned with elaborately worked coin silver, set off a new round of teasing among the retirees. "You didn't get those here, did you?" several laughed.

In 1906 the Denver Mint struck 167 million coins. Today that's about an average week's production.

Chapter Notes

1. Details of the inside of the Denver Mint come from our December 2005 private tour with Guillermo Hernandez, public affairs director at the Denver Mint.

2. The sexual harassment complaints were covered extensively by the *Denver Post* and *Rocky Mountain News* in 2003. The *Wall Street Journal* published a long story on March 22, 2006. The official Mint statement is from a joint release of the US Mint and Class Counsel, posted in the US Mint Pressroom on March 31, 2006. The *Denver Post* reported details of the settlement on April 1, 2006.

3. Information about security at the Denver Mint is primarily from a telephone interview in October 2005 with William F. Daddio, associate director for protection/ chief of US Mint Police. Mr. Daddio was very candid in sharing his security concerns with us, although he refused to divulge the alarm codes for the vault.

4. The story about Teddy Roosevelt and Saint-Gaudens comes from the Senate Banking Committee Coin Design Symposium. Speeches from that symposium are available online at http://banking.senate.gov/coin2000/coin-sym.htm.

5. The Wisconsin State Quarter anomalies burst into the news in April 2005 as media from MSNBC to *USA Today* reported the story of the extra leaves. We spoke to numismatists and coin dealers about the value of the coins and their speculation as to the cause of the error. *USA Today* obtained the official report of the Treasury Department's Office of Inspector General through a Freedom of Information Act request. *USA Today* reported those results on January 20, 2006.

"Coins are an important part of our society and they define who we are. When we pick up a coin, we're holding history in the palm of our hand."
—Jay Johnson, 36th director of the US Mint

Glossary

Alloy: a mixture of at least two metals used to manufacture coins

American Numismatic Association (ANA): a nonprofit educational organization for the study of money throughout the world

Annealing: the process by which blanks (planchets) are heated in a furnace, then cooled, to soften the metal while maintaining its strength

Assay: to analyze and determine the purity of metal

Bag mark: a mark on a coin from contact with other coins in a mint bag

Blank: the round piece of metal that, when struck with a design, becomes a coin; also called a planchet

Bullion: platinum, gold, or silver in the form of bars or other storage shapes (coins or ingots)

Business strike: a coin produced for mass circulation

Clad coinage: coins with outer layers and core made of different nonprecious metals. Since 1965, all circulating US dimes, quarters, half-dollars, and dollars have been clad. Also called sandwich coins

Collar: a metal piece that holds the expanding metal of a planchet as it is struck

Commemorative: a special coin or medal issued to honor an outstanding person, place or event

Designer: the artist who creates a coin's design. An engraver actually makes the dies

Die: an engraved steel stamp that strikes a design upon a blank piece of metal to make a coin

Edge: the outer border of a coin, considered the "third side" (not to be confused with "rim"), which may be reeded, flat, or otherwise

Engraver: an artist who sculpts a model of a coin's design in bas relief

Error: an improperly produced coin, overlooked in production, and later released into circulation

Face value: the legal tender value of a coin

Field: that part of a coin's surface not used for design or inscription

Inscription: words stamped on a coin or medal

Legend: principal lettering on a coin

Motto: a word, sentence, or phrase inscribed on a coin to express a guiding national principle. For example, *E Pluribus Unum* inscribed on all US circulating coins is Latin for "out of many, one"

Numismatics: the study and collecting of things that are used as money, including coins, tokens, paper bills, and medals

Obverse: the "heads" side of a coin, usually marked with the date, mintmark, and main design

Planchet: the rimmed, round piece of metal on which a coin design is struck

Proof: a specially produced coin made from burnished planchets and dies struck more than once to sharpen the design. These high-relief coins are the finest examples of coins.

Proof set: a complete set of proof coins of each denomination struck in a year

Relief: the part of a coin's design that is raised above the surface, opposite of incuse

Restrike: a coin that is minted using the original dies but at a later date

Reverse: "tails" side of a coin

Riddler: a machine that screens out blanks (planchets) that are the wrong size or shape

Rim: the raised edge on both sides of a coin (created by the upsetting mill) that helps protect the coin's design from wear

Sheet: strip of alloyed metal from which blanks are punched

Strike: the process of stamping a coin blank with a design. The strength of the imprint—full, average, or weak—affects the value of rare coins

Token: metal object resembling a coin

Uncirculated: the term "uncirculated" has multiple meanings when applied to a coin. It can describe the manufacturing process, serve as an evaluation or grade of a coin's preservation and quality, or it can mean that the coin has never been used in commerce. Uncirculated collectible coins are produced in Denver and Philadelphia using the same process as circulating coins but with quality enhancements, such as slightly higher coining force, early strikes from dies, burnished planchets, and special packaging. Uncirculated coins may vary to some degree because of blemishes, toning, or slight imperfections. In 2005 the US Mint began producing uncirculated collector's sets with a satin finish to distinguish the coins.

Upsetting mill: a machine that pushes up the metal to form the rim on both sides of a blank (planchet)

Webbing: the metal left over after blanks have been punched. It is recycled to make more coins

Bibliography and Resources

Bibliography

American Numismatic Association's (ANA) monthly journal, *The Numismatist*, provided many articles that we used as background and source materials, going back to volume 33, March 1920. The most useful way to approach the ANA journal is to search online at the Dwight N. Manley Library at the American Numismatic Association Money Museum in Colorado Springs. Our search criteria were Denver + Mint.

ANA. *Oops! Mistakes on Money Educator Workbook*. Colorado Springs, Colorado: American Numismatic Association, 2005.

Arps, Louisa Ward. *Denver in Slices*. Denver: Sage Press, 1998.

Congressional Budget Office. *H. R. 902 Presidential $1 Coin Act of 2005*, Cost Estimate, April 12, 2005.

Denver Mint. *Just Look for the "D"* video, Denver Mint, 1995.

Eitemiller, David. *Historic Tours: The Denver Mint.* Frederick, Colorado: Jende-Hagan Book Corporation, 1983.

Goodstein, Phil. *The Seamy Side of Denver.* Denver: New Social Publications, 1993.

Jones, William C., and Kenton Forrest. *Denver, a Pictorial History from Frontier Camp to Queen City of the Plains.* Boulder, Colorado: Pruett Publishing, 1973.

Leach, Frank. *Recollections of a Newspaper Man—A Record of Life and Events in California.* San Francisco: Samuel Levinson, 1917.

Lee, Lawrence. *Secrets of the Denver Mint Archives* video, Boulder Media Resources Corporation, 2003.

Mumey, Nolie. *Clark, Gruber and Company, 1860–1865, a Pioneer Denver Mint, History of Their Coinage.* Denver: Artcraft Press, 1950.

Muonio, Anna. "Mint Condition," *Fast Company*, Issue 30, December 1999.

Murphy, Jack A. *Geology Tour of Denver's Buildings and Monuments.* Denver: Historic Denver, Inc., and Denver Museum of Natural History, 1995. pp. 6-21, 28-29.

Noel, Thomas J., and Barbara S. Norgren. *Denver, the City Beautiful and Its Architects, 1893–1941.* Denver: Historic Denver, Inc., 1987. pp. 1-26.

Ohanian, Susan. *Denver Mint: Fun Facts and Figures about Making Coins in Colorado.* Columbus, Ohio: SRA/McGraw-Hill, 1996.

Parkhill, Forbes. "Pioneer Denver Mint Robbery," *The Denver Westerners Monthly Roundup*, Vol. XIII, No. 7, July 1957. pp. 5-20.

Rapsus, Ginger. *The United States Clad Coinage.* Wolfeboro, New Hampshire: Bowers and Merena Galleries, 1992.

Swails, Alfred J. *World War II Remembered, History in Your Hands, a Numismatic Study.* Port Clinton, Ohio: BNR Press, 1983.

US Mint. *50 States Commemorative Coin Program Study.* Coopers & Lybrand, May 30, 1997.

US Mint, *Annual Report,* 2004. Washington, DC, US Government.

US Mint, *Strategic Plan 2002–2007.* Washington, DC, US Government.

Libraries and Museums

These resources are available online. However, if you can visit and talk with the knowledgeable librarians and researchers, you will be rewarded. Their passion for their field and for history is a joy to be around.

Denver Public Library, Western History Department Central Library
10 W. Fourteenth Ave. Pkwy.
Denver, CO 80204
720-865-1111

www.denverlibrary.org

This is a boundless resource with more than 600,000 historic photographs. The library Web site features "Ask a Librarian" where you can ask research questions online and a real live Denver librarian will answer. Materials in the western history department cannot be checked out, but the reading room is comfortable and beautiful and the copier is fast and clean.

Colorado Historical Society
1300 Broadway
Denver, Colorado 80203
303-866-3682

www.coloradohistory.org

Knowledgeable historians and librarians help with research done onsite. An extensive, easily searchable photo archive is available.

American Numismatic Association Money Museum and Dwight N. Manley Numismatic Library
818 North Cascade Avenue
Colorado Springs, CO 80903-3279
719-632-2646

www.money.org

Some materials may be checked out to members or requested by Colorado libraries. Others are for use on the premises. The museum also has an extensive photo archive.

Web Sites

http://banking.senate.gov/coin2000/coin-sym.htm

Senate Banking Committee Coin Design Symposium was held September 2000.

www.bls.gov

The Bureau of Labor Statistics site offers information on the changing value of money.

BIBLIOGRAPHY AND RESOURCES

www.coinbooks.org

The Numismatic Bibliomania Society (NBS) is a nonprofit educational organization founded in 1980 to support and promote the use and collecting of numismatic literature. Numismatic literature includes books, periodicals, catalogs, and other written or printed material relating to coins, medals, tokens, or paper money, ancient or modern, US or worldwide. Membership is open to any individual or organization interested in the study of numismatics and the study and collecting of numismatic literature.

www.coinfacts.com

Information for coin collectors and anyone interested in coinage.

www.coinpage.com

This site is intended to provide high-quality coin and coin-related images for public use. It is a tremendous resource that invites collectors, dealers, and photographers to post their images as well. Many of the photos we used from Coin Page were provided for use by coin dealers. You can find their offerings on eBay.

www.coinworld.com

Numismatic magazine's Web site.

www.money.org

The Web site for the American Numismatic Association.

Highlights include a fully searchable library catalog (you can even e-mail the librarian, who answers promptly), educational materials you can download, museum news, and a market to purchase books or supplies.

www.pcgs.com

The Web site of Professional Coin Grading Service is a veritable feast of information about coins and their history.

www.usmint.gov

The official Web site for the US Mint. You can take virtual tours of the Mints in Denver and Philadelphia, learn about circulating, commemorative and historic coins, check out the business of making coins, and download educational materials. This should be the first stop for anyone wanting to learn more about American coinage.

Index

INDEX

Easy Order Form
CHECK YOUR LEADING BOOKSTORE
OR ORDER HERE

Item	Quantity	Price

Please include $1 shipping for each order.
Colorado residents add 7% sales tax.

_____ My check or money order for $_____ is enclosed.
_____ Please charge my credit card.

Name_____

Organization_____

Address_____

City/State/Zip_____

Phone_____E-mail_____

_____ MasterCard _____ Visa _____ Discover

Card #_____

Exp. Date_____

Signature_____

Please make your check payable and return to:

Mapletree Publishing Company
6233 Harvard Lane
Highlands Ranch, CO 80130
Call your credit card order to: 800-537-0414
Fax: 303-791-9028
Secure online ordering: www.mapletreepublishing.com